Hamlyn all-colour paperbacks

Michael Hardwick

Discovery of
Japan

Illustrated by
Michael Shoebridge

Hamlyn · London
Sun Books · Melbourne

FOREWORD

To her Asian neighbours, China and Korea, Japan owes much in terms of language, religion, arts and crafts. The Western nations brought her industry, commerce and other vital institutions which have led to the highest living standard in the East and made her one of the world's most dynamic communities.

Much of Japan's greatness has been thrust upon her. Having repulsed early attacks from Asia but willingly absorbed the invasions of knowledge and culture, she was 'discovered' by the West in the sixteenth century and thought to continue the process. When the West wanted too much of its own way, Japan ruthlessly severed relations with the world, with remarkable results upon her cultural life but at the cost of a share in international progress.

In the mid-nineteenth century she was compelled by the West to abandon her feudal ways, so determined to learn all she could and then, by the application of native genius, rise supreme; but ambitious militarism precipitated her into disaster.

Profiting by her links with the West in recent years of Asian upheaval, she has again rocketed to prosperity and new influence in both hemispheres. This book seeks to reflect this unique pattern of events.

Published by The Hamlyn Publishing Group Limited
London · New York · Sydney · Toronto
Hamlyn House, Feltham, Middlesex, England
In association with Sun Books Pty Ltd Melbourne

Copyright © The Hamlyn Publishing Group Limited 1970

SBN 600 002799

Phototypeset by Jolly & Barber Limited, Rugby, Warwickshire
Colour separations by Schwitter Limited, Zurich
Printed in England by Sir Joseph Causton & Sons Limited

CONTENTS

BIRTH AND EARLY HISTORY

For Japan to be known as 'The Land of the Rising Sun' is no mere poetic fancy. The sun figures prominently in Japanese mythology and religion, both of which have shaped the people's character.

Flags showing the rising sun were used by some leading clans more than 600 years ago but the present flag, Hinomaru – 'Round the Sun' – was officially adopted only in 1870, after the visit of Commodore Perry's squadron had ended Japan's isolation from the world and it became obvious that in future Japanese ships should carry national identification. Curiously enough the first ship to fly it was a U.S. Navy cruiser, the *Powhattan*, in 1860, when she was placed at the disposal of the first diplomatic delegation ever sent abroad by the Japanese government.

Japan's fine national anthem, 'Kimigayo' ('Reign of our Emperor') also owes something to the West. The words, part of an ancient poem, were given in 1860 to an Englishman, John William Fenton, who was serving the Japanese Army as its first bandmaster. He set it to a tune which was used for twenty years until a Japanese Court musician composed a new version for traditional Japanese instruments. For international use this was harmonized by Fenton's German successor, Franz Eckert, according to the Gregorian scale which is the basis of Western mediaeval church music.

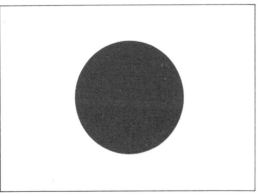

Right:
The tower-keep of Hirosaki Castle seen through its famous cherry-blossom

MANCHURIA

CHINA

KOREA

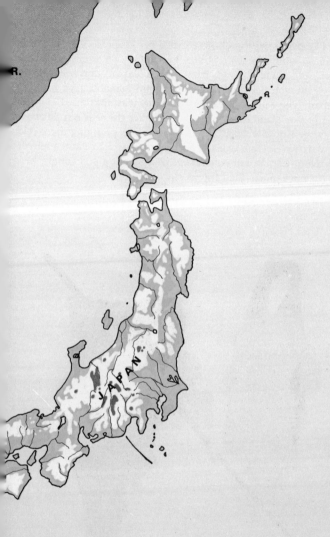

Japan's four main islands and thousands of islets comprise a total
area of 142,726 square miles, less than one-twentieth the area of
the U.S.A. and about half as much again as the United Kingdom:
yet her population is about 100 million, nearly twice that of the U.K.
Tokyo alone has a population of over eleven million.

In early times the Chinese called her Zippon – 'Origin of the Sun' – which became Nihon or Nippon. Western travellers used the name Zipangu from which 'Japan' derives. Legend says the god and goddess Izanagi and Izanami gave birth to Japan. The Sun-goddess, Amaterasu, was appointed ruler of the heavens and her Storm brother over the seas but he acted so violently that Amaterasu hid in a cave, plunging the world into darkness. In a tree the gods hung a necklace and a mirror to tempt her. When Amaterasu peeped out a god caught her. Light once more filled the world.

The God and Goddess Izanagi and Izanami

Amaterasu's rebellious brother, Susanowo, was banished to the 'Land of Darkness' – the earth. In Japan he killed a monster, and found in one of its eight tails a sword, which he gave to Amaterasu as a peace-offering. So the Imperial Regalia of Japan consists of a sword, a mirror and a necklace.

Amaterasu's grandson Ninigo-no-Mikoto, equipped with these treasures descended to rule Japan. His great-grandson, Jimmu Tenno, became the first 'human' Emperor in 660 B.C., hence the belief, held firmly by all Japanese until quite recently, in the divine ancestry of their Emperors.

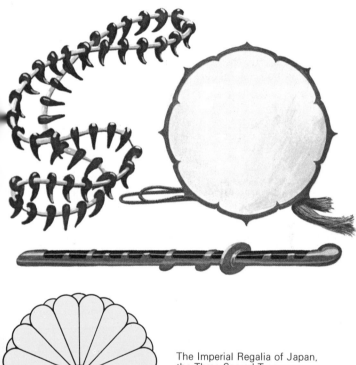

The Imperial Regalia of Japan, the Three Sacred Treasures, consists of this sword, the mirror and the necklace; (left) the Imperial Crest – a sixteen-petal chrysanthemum

Until the end of the Second World War Japanese children in their first years at primary school were taught the myths of their country's creation as truths and any teacher rash enough to throw doubt on them risked losing his job. Beliefs have changed now, yet the apt symbolism of the legends – the triumph of sun over storm but only after she has been coaxed to return in springtime from her winter's hiding in the cave – remains a living element in Japan's most widespread religion, Shinto, 'The Way of the Gods'.

The actual origins of Japan and her people are not precisely known. The original inhabitants seem to have been the race which now survives in dwindling numbers in the northern island of Hokkaido, the Ainus. Pure Ainus – and there are very few of them left – are quite different from Japanese. Japanese have scant facial hair: the 'Hairy Ainus' are the hairiest race in the world. They do not have Mongolian features, their doleful eyes seeming to belong to the Caucasus. They worship nature and especially bears, which they sacrifice at solemn festivals. Once they were great warriors. It took the Japanese centuries to subdue them. Now they are a sad minority, a race that has lost almost everything but its name. Japan's closeness to Asia makes it virtually certain that her first population came from there, from China and Manchuria, by way of Korea. They settled into village communities in good areas for rice-growing to practise the farming knowledge they had brought.

In the middle of the fourth century A.D. the Empress Jingo organized a military expedition to Korea which resulted in a Japanese colony being established on the tip of the Korean peninsula. This link was to have immediate and tremendous consequences. One was the importation of the Chinese form of writing, though for many years it spread no further than the Japanese Imperial Court. Spoken Chinese and Japanese differ greatly, yet the Japanese script is essentially Chinese to this day and newspapers sometimes print marginal notes explaining the meaning of a complicated character. Also from Korea – or through there from other parts of Asia – came whole communities of workers skilled with metals and ceramics and in cultivating silkworms. They settled in Japan and founded an artistic and cultural heritage unsurpassed in the world.

Above:
The Empress
Jingo
Below:
Early artefacts

One of the most important arrivals from the Asian continent was Buddhism which came to Japan in about the middle of the sixth century. It never supplanted Shinto but complemented it, so that most Japanese are now both Buddhists and Shintoists. Buddhism was strongly opposed at first for fear it might endanger the worship of Japan's own gods. But it came at a time of great clan rivalry. The powerful Soga clan decided it would be prudent to support Buddhism, and, after some wavering, the Imperial Family followed suit. So Buddhism became accepted despite the outbreak of an epidemic which was widely interpreted as due to the wrath of the Japanese gods at this intrusion on their exclusive domain. Shinto did not precede Buddhism by more than a century and only got its name when Buddhism arrived.

Buddhism has always had the ascendancy. There is more devotion to it in Japan than in India, Buddha's birthplace. In the early stages of its history in Japan it exercised a powerful civilizing influence, and much of the best literature and art has been inspired by it or executed by its priests.

Shinto is centred on the

Figure of a Buddhist saint

worship of nature and one's ancestors and lays great stress on purity and purification, with much worship and bathing by priests and believers. It is a rather light-hearted, free-and-easy religion, with no set day of worship and no restrictive rules about celibacy or what not to eat or drink. It has more than 80,000 shrines all over Japan, ranging from little ones in the home or by the wayside to the Grand Shrine of Ise, which millions visit as a sort of Japanese Mecca. Shinto has given the Japanese people a mixture of virtues and vices: a worldly outlook, a contempt for death, and, instead of repentance, a habit of washing away moral uncleanliness and sin.

Above:
Shinto shrine — a modern reproduction of the Grand Shrine at Ise

Below: Buddhist shrine

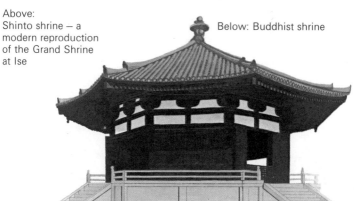

13

The cause of Buddhism owed much of its advance to the learned, cultivated and much loved young Regent, Prince Shotoku, who grasped its precepts better than anyone and furthered its cause, declaring that no state could manage its affairs properly without considering the principles of Confucianism, Buddhism and Shinto. Heeding this parties of scholars and officials began paying visits to China from where the two former had reached Japan. It was the time of the brilliant T'ang dynasty (A.D. 618–906), the marvel of all Asia. The visiting Japanese, showing that now familiar Japanese aptitude for borrowing and adapting foreign ideas and techniques, gained much of artistic, religious and political value from China, including an elaborate system of central government which was applied to Japan by Fujiwara Kamatari who had overthrown the Soga clan. Arrogant and ambitious, the Soga had precipitated their own downfall. Their head, Soga no Iruka, had assumed rule of the country, a move which Kamatari saw as a threat to the whole system of Solar Dignity. Soga was cut down at court and his clan's influence toppled with him.

Largely due to the new governmental system the Fujiwara

The Shoso-in (below) is a storehouse containing a remarkable collection of furniture, ornaments and belongings of the Imperial family in eighth century Nara.

The Kasuga Shrine (above), founded in 768 as the shrine of the Fujiwara family, is reached along an avenue of some 2,000 ancient stone lanterns.

family was able to hold the real power in Japan for some four centuries. Until the year 710 Japan had no fixed place of residence for the Imperial family. With each new Emperor the capital had also changed. In this year what was intended to be a permanent capital was established at Nara, though it served for only seventy-four years, during which time the Imperial family's authority extended to cover the whole country. Many great and exquisite temples, palaces and houses were built at Nara. Some of them remain as the best examples of T'ang architecture to be seen today.

Nara was laid out on the plan of the T'ang capital of China and was soon attracting scholarly visitors from many parts of Asia. They found a remarkable agglomeration of architectural and artistic creations, strongly influenced by Chinese and Indian models but already showing evidence of much originality. They also found Nara to be a veritable Buddhist stronghold with seven important monasteries in or close to the city. Because Nara had become so Buddhist-dominated the Imperial Court moved from there to establish another capital in the new city of Kyoto in 794. Another name for Kyoto is Heian-kyo, 'Capital of Peace', and for the most part the so-called Heian period (794–1185) was one of peace, presided over by the Fujiwara family, now linked by marriage with the Imperial Family and, to all intents and purposes, ruling the country. During the ninth–eleventh centuries Japan's contacts with China, Korea and the rest of Asia dwindled, and from the sophisticated, languid court circle there burst a spectacular surge of artistic and cultural achievement which now owed as much to Japanese taste and skill as to foreign models. The cultural life was limited to a small, aristocratic circle but its effects, transmitted over the years to the Japanese people as a whole, gave them a legacy of respect for formality of expression and for the application of art to everyday life that has made them one of the world's most cultivated and courteous peoples.

This life of exquisite formality lived at the court of the Heian period gave rise to some of the masterpieces of Japanese literature, many of them written by women. Male writers traditionally preferred to use the Chinese language; but the women, aristocrats of great taste and keen appreciation of beauty, used the recently invented kana, a syllabary able to capture the sound of Japanese far better than Chinese characters could. A new literary form were the monogatari, prose tales with some poetic elements. One of these, Genji Monogatari (*The Tale of Genji*), written by a court lady, Murasaki Shikibu, in the middle of the Heian period, is Japan's best-known contribution to world literature and is claimed to be the first novel ever. It is a romance about Prince Genji, his ladies, his children and grandchildren, and it is full of delightfully observed studies of the circle in which the author moved.

Buddhism had widespread effects on Japanese art and architecture. It came as a form of magic to a lot of people and the many sculptured and painted images it produced were believed to possess powers of soothing, healing or wrath. This 'Healing Buddha' (*right*), Yakushi Nyorai, was carved from wood in the ninth century. Japan has always been extensively forested and wood has been the basic material for sculpture and building. The much-used hinoki (cypress) is so durable that a great many ancient statues and buildings can still be seen. It was during the Heian period that the traditional Japanese style of building gave way to the familiar gracefully curving roofs of slate, such as on the Pagoda of Daigoji, built at Kyoto in A.D. 951 (*top right*).

Another art form derived from China but brought to perfection in Japan at this time was hand scroll painting, telling a story in almost moving-picture form. The artist's skill carries the eye swiftly and smoothly from scene to scene. *Right* is a detail from one of three famous scrolls illustrating the Heiji civil wars. These were painted in the thirteenth century.

Right:
The Pagoda of
Daigoji, Kyoto

Left: Warrior in contemporary armour

Right:
Yoritomo

Though the Heian Court circle had gained in sophistication, the ordinary people had acquired only new masters and increasing taxes. Aristocrats sampling the delights of Kyoto left ambitious chieftains to run their estates, while tax-exempt Buddhist communities attracted peasants to their lands, took their taxes and grew richer and more influential. Private armies began to be raised, unchecked by the government which saw them as potentially useful in case of war. But when war did come, in the twelfth century, it was among the Fujiwaras themselves, quarrelling over political appointments. The rival factions called in the help of private armies, among them those belonging to the Minamoto and Taira clans. After bloody fighting the Fujiwaras found that in settling their differences for them the Taira and Minamoto had taken control of the country. The Taira were the first to gain power and kept it ruthlessly for twenty-five years, establishing a separate capital at Kamakura. But in 1185 they were beaten in a great sea battle in the Shimonoseki Straits by the Minomoto, led by Yoshitsune, who, it has been claimed, later fled to Asia to

escape his brother's disfavour and became none less than Genghis Khan.

It was this elder brother of Yoshitsune, Yoritomo, who set up at Kamakura the Bakufu, an unashamedly military system of government. He was given the appointment of Shogun, or Generalissimo, by the thirteen-year-old Emperor. He posted samurai warriors as police and tax-collectors in every district, and so began that dual system of rule by Emperor and Shogun which would last in Japan for seven centuries. After Yoritomo had died in 1199 and power passed to his widow's family, the Hojo, Japan faced her first peril from outside. In 1274 Kublai Khan, the Mongolian emperor who had seized the Chinese throne and subdued Korea, moved to seize some islands between Kyushu and Korea. The small garrisons resisted to the death. The Mongols returned with a bigger force in 1281 but after fifty-three days fighting, a typhoon suddenly wiped out the entire Mongol fleet. Japan was saved and the typhoon hailed as a Divine Wind – Kamikaze, a word which would be invoked in a vastly different fight for survival seven centuries later.

Dai-Batsu Buddha at Kamakura

Buddhist and Shinto priests gained much prestige for the prayers which were believed to have prompted this divine intervention against the Mongols, while the Shogunate, which had led the actual fighting, gained no credit because it could not reward its warriors. Japan was impoverished. Bad harvests and epidemics had brought the peasants close to starvation. The forces of Go-Daigo, an ex-Emperor whom the Hojo family had deposed, overran Kamakura and the last Hojo regent and hundreds of his followers committed mass suicide.

Buddhism is a religion of many sects – today there are eleven in Japan, subdivided into fifty-eight branches. Three great ones which arose during the Kamakura period were Jodo-Shinshu, Nichiren and Zen. All became quickly popular, the last because it seemed particularly applicable to the Japanese blend of warrior-aesthete-scholar. It taught indifference to suffering or pleasure and called for self-discipline and medita-

Buddhist-influenced scroll painting

tion in order to achieve close unity with nature, leading to sublime enlightenment. These more peaceful aspects of Zen have made it newly popular in our own time.

Zen Buddhism also had a strong influence on art, especially paintings of nature, landscapes, portraits and historical scenes on scrolls.

Another art to reach perfection at this time was that of the swordsmith. Two hundred years before the forging in Europe of such classic blades as the Toledo and Ferrara, Japanese swordsmiths were making exquisite swords whose quality and artistry have never been equalled. A secret process enabled the cutting edge to be made so sharp that it was dangerous even to touch, while the back remained soft enough to resist breakage when used against armour. As the sun is a national symbol to Japan, so is the sword, synonymous with good faith and the suppression of evil forces.

The Emperor Go-Daigo was soon deposed by his former ally Ashikaga Takauji, of the house of Minamoto, who set up on the throne a member of another Imperial line, Kamyo, who in turn recognized Ashikaga as Shogun. Ashikaga had established his Shogunate at Muromachi, a district of Kyoto, so the period covered by the Shogunate of the Ashikaga family – 1339-1573 – is known as the Muromachi era. It was not a happy time. The Shoguns lived in Kyoto, practising sophisticated arts and ceremonials amidst surroundings of great luxury, while all over the country barons fought and bandits took advantage of the decay of military families and seized their lands. The Shogunate was indolent and helpless. The Emperors were in such reduced circumstances that one of them had to go into the streets of Kyoto and sell examples of his calligraphy in order to raise cash.

Kinkakuji Temple, Kyoto, built 1394 by Yoshimitsu

Paradoxically it was a time of some social progress, economic development and a further great flowering of culture. Although taxation in the provinces was harsh and dissatisfaction widespread, the 1,000-year-old serfdom of the peasants was ended and local rulers had to pay some regard to rights and conditions if they wanted to recruit followers. A breed of Japanese pirates had appeared; but so, too, had peaceful seafarers, who began to trade with China. A number of quite busy ports came into being on the Japanese coast, through which were exported manufactured goods and imported such useful items as copper coins to increase the use of coinage in place of rice as Japan's currency. The most important arrival was further Chinese influence on the arts and culture. Though they owe so much to Chinese origin or influence, such enduring classic features of Japanese culture as the Noh drama, the Tea Ceremony, flower arrangement and landscape gardening were chiefly developed in this time.

One of 1,001 images of Goddess of Mercy in Myohin Temple, Kyoto

25

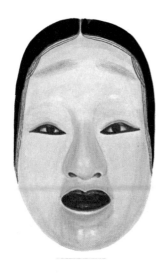

Masks for Noh

Noh drama is difficult to follow in its detail but its overall effect can be almost hypnotically appealing to Westerners prepared to surrender their minds to the slow-moving spectacle of symbolically posturing figures against sparse but ingeniously effective settings. The eerie chanting of the characters is heightened by that of the chorus kneeling beside the stage, as it comments on the action and describes the change of scenes, and the tap and wail of three drums and a flute. Since all emotion must be conveyed by posture and mimic gesture, the performers wear masks symbolizing the type of character each is playing. Many of these masks have been handed down through the ages and in their own right are most desirable collectors' pieces. Noh was originally performed exclusively for the upper classes, and its following has always been limited. The traditions of Noh are kept alive by its performers, many of whom come from a hereditary line of Noh artists. The number of Western admirers of Noh is growing and there have been performances at several important international festivals of the arts.

Scene from a Noh drama

Noh is the oldest of the three major forms of classical Japanese drama, tracing its origins back to the thirteenth century when certain Buddhist rituals and dances of the preceding eras were integrated and developed. Indeed Noh is believed to be a Buddhist term referring to unity between arts and between artists and audience. This is what it seeks to achieve, being in fact neither drama nor dance, but a fusion of both, together with stylized music and the chanting by the actors of rigidly formalized phrases, each as a rule of five or seven syllables. Though it is not necessarily 'religious' in content, a priest is always one of the characters, and the 'hero' or 'heroine' generally achieves the blessed state of Nirvana. The Noh stage is much smaller than that of ordinary theatres and has a roof within the roof of the main building in perpetuation of the fact that Noh was originally performed out of doors. About 1,000 Noh plays are said to have been composed, of which total only about one quarter still remain in performance.

Tea first reached Japan from China in about A.D. 700, though matcha, the powdered green tea used in the ceremony, did not arrive until some 500 years later. In the fourteenth century a tea game – tocha – came from China. Guests at a tea party had to identify the best type. This stimulated the growth of tea in Japan and moved certain formal-minded men to transform a party game into an elaborate ceremonial, with strictly defined utensils and movements, calculated to promote calmness, grace and contemplation. A Zen Buddhist priest, Sen Rikyu (1521–1591), perfected it to the form it has kept ever since. It teaches the participants to notice simple and pleasing objects, to derive satisfaction from them and to extend courtesy towards one another and to those inanimate objects which play their part in our lives. The ceremony (chanoyu) can last as long as four hours and often takes place in a special small tea house in a wooded section of a formal garden. At each stage the quietly clothed guests inspect and admire the simple setting in which they are kneeling, the few ornaments and decorations and the tea utensils and, of course, the taste of the thick or thin green tea.

Sen Rikyu, the inventor of the tea ceremony

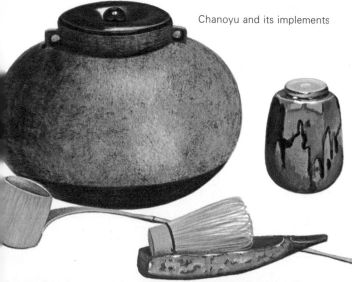

Chanoyu and its implements

Ikebana, flower arrangement, has probably had more influence on the Western world than any other Japanese art form apart from the ukiyoe colour print. Its principles spring from philosophical Buddhist concepts of unity with nature, though the religious element has by now given way to sheer love of form. Western flower-fanciers mostly admire the lushness and colouring of a bloom. Ikebana rejects this, concentrating upon the stark beauty of a flowing line. Full blooms are seldom used, for their perfection quickly fades, symbolizing the past, death and dissolution. Tight buds are much preferred. They stand for future promise; they do not interfere with the line of the stem or branch; and their slow opening offers continuing stages of delight. Heaven, Man and Earth form the framework of Ikebana. Heaven is symbolized by the stem which forms the central line of the arrangement and rises highest. Man comes second in prominence extending sideways and forward of the centre line. The shortest stem, to the front or slightly to the opposite side of the roots of the other two, stands for Earth.

The art of gardening

reached Japan from China. Rigid rules give each feature its own significance – a small hill standing for a religious principle, a philosophical point being made through the curve of a bridge over a stream which might be of water or merely of sand or gravel. Garden designs are classed as elaborate, intermediate and abbreviated. There are ten or more ways of arranging a waterfall and countless permutations of the placing of stones, trees, bridges and islands to allow the eye to travel effortlessly from feature to feature, or to be caught by some unexpected vista that will bring to mind a harmonious parallel with life or thought. The Meiji Restoration (1868) brought the destruction of many fine formal gardens in an eagerness to break with the feudal past and embrace the new. Attempts were made to introduce Western-style gardening, with little success. Nothing suits Japan's terrain and architecture like a Japanese-style garden, however simply contrived, and the harmony that can be achieved and the accompanying sense of tranquility have to be experienced to be appreciated.

This is a plan (*right*) of a 'hill garden', a type featuring one or more hills, a pond and a stream, intended to be contemplated from the parlour of the house (at the bottom of the plan). In the foreground is the pond, approached by stepping stones of carefully chosen shapes, and divided into separate areas, each with different characteristics, by promontories and little

Plan of 'Sin' (Elaborate) Style of Hiu Garden

1. Verandah

2. 'Takizoe-no-isi', 'Stones of Both Sides of Waterfall'

3. 'Raihai-Seki' or 'Worshipping Stone', placed in central position for worshipping gods

4. 'Syôzô-Seki' or 'Perfect View Stone', responding to the views in the landscape

5. 'Garan-Seki' or 'Pedestal Stone', at the parting of stepping-stones, originally the foundation stone of the temple

6. 'Syôsin-Boku', principle tree to be planted as the focus to the view

7. 'Keiyô-Boku' or 'View Perfecting Tree', in a different form from 6

8. 'Tyôzu-Bati' or 'Water Basin'

9. 'Kutunugi-Isi' or 'Stone where shoes are taken off'

humped bridges. Hills of increasing height carry the eye up to the largest one, at top left, before which stands the principal tree, the focal point of the whole effect.

ACCEPTANCE AND REJECTION OF THE WEST

In the middle of the sixteenth century the West and Japan came into conjunction for the first time. They were brought together when a ship from Macao, the Portuguese trading base in China, was driven ashore on an island near Kyushu. The crew, the first Europeans to set foot in Japan, were warmly received and soon afterwards ships from Macao began to call at the Kyushu ports, some merchants crossing to Honshu, as far as Kyoto. Of all the goods the Portuguese brought none was more welcomed than the smooth-bore musket. The Japanese quickly learned to make their own, characteristically going one better by decorating their weapons superbly and elevating the gunsmith's craft, like the swordsmith's, to an art form. Guns were soon being manufactured in many parts of Japan but principally in a district of central Honshu dominated by a fearless, ruthless daimyo, or feudal lord, Nobunaga. The musket arrived at exactly the right moment for this ambitious man. Using it he was able to bring nearly half of Japan's sixty-six provinces under his control. He also made effective use of another new arrival, Christianity. In 1549 the Portuguese Jesuit missionary Francis Xavier reached Kyushu in a Japanese privateer's vessel. The Christian teaching he brought with him was well received by the Japanese. Many converts were made and feudal lords declared their support, though some for reasons more material than spiritual. Nobunaga, annoyed with the Buddhists who had aligned themselves with some of his rivals, assisted the missionaries who came after Francis

St Francis Xavier
Left: Japanese with gun

Xavier and helped them spread their faith throughout Japan.

The Christians saw only the purest motives in Nobunaga's interest. He genuinely admired their crusading spirit but used them cleverly as a counter to the militaristic influence of Buddhism. He did not live to finish unifying the whole country under himself. He built a fine castle and a 'navy' of six ships, larger than any seen in Japan before, and, it is said, planned to conquer China. He died aged forty-nine through the treachery of an officer who bore him a grudge and attacked Nobunaga's personal force at a temple in Kyoto. The guard were cut down and Nobunaga, badly wounded, committed suicide.

Fortunately an oustanding man was ready to step into Nobunaga's place. He was a romantic figure of humble origins, Hideyoshi, 'the Japanese Napoleon'. His father had been an ordinary soldier and Hideyoshi had served as Nobunaga's groom. He was almost a dwarf, notably ugly, but of compelling charm and strength. He quickly put down the faction that had killed Nobunaga, then subdued the feuding barons so that within eight years all Japan was at peace, an efficient central administration was operating, a national land survey was under way and Hideyoshi's great castle of Osaka, which took thousands of men three years to build, was completed. Hideyoshi made friends with potential enemies and placed loyal supporters in territories between barons likely to fight one another. He would have liked to be Shogun but could not; but he got the Emperor to grant him the title of kampaku or civil dictator. Anyone opposing him became technically a rebel against the Emperor. Conscious of his lowly birth and wishing to achieve greatness in all eyes, Hideyoshi decided to conquer China. The King of Korea refused to let his troops pass through that country, so he invaded it, moving swiftly over Pusan, Seoul, the Imjin River and Pyong-yang. But the Chinese came to Korea's aid. The invaders were driven back in winter conditions and forced to evacuate. Another attempt was made several years later but was unsuccessful. All these campaigns achieved was to bring much hardship and distress to the Korean people and establish a legacy of hatred for the Japanese. Some of Hideyoshi's generals had displayed the Christian Cross on their war banners. Christianity continued to flourish and relations remained good between the Japanese and the small Western community. But the late sixteenth century saw Spanish friars coming to join the Portuguese Jesuits. Neither liked the other. As they bickered, a Spanish seaman's boast that the Spanish empire overseas had been founded largely upon the pioneering of the missionary friars reached Hideyoshi's ears, making him suspect a Spanish plot to take over Japan. By way of a caution he arrested many of the friars' converts and sentenced to death twenty-six Christians, though leaving the Jesuits alone. The victims were martyred by the Japanese form of crucifixion at Nagasaki in 1597, the year before Hideyoshi's own death from an unremarkable illness.

Above: Hideyoshi

Below: Memorial to martyrs at Nagasaki

Will Adams
and (right) his shrine

Far right: A seventeenth-century
Dutch ship

Hideyoshi's son, Hideyori, was only five and Hideyoshi had arranged for a council of guardians to care for him. One of these was a man who would soon prove himself as outstanding as Hideyoshi himself and Nobunaga before him. This was Tokugawa Iyeyasu, of the Shogunate household of Minamoto. Cleverer than his two great predecessors, he was a skilled judge of the character and ability of other men, so that he was able to avoid mistaken alliances and he possessed a degree of patient cunning that brought him eventually what he wanted. Before long he was scheming to get rid of the little Hideyori, overcome his supporters and persuade the Emperor to appoint him Shogun.

While Iyeyasu was containing himself in patience a Dutch vessel limped into a Japanese port in distress. Only a quarter of her crew survived, including a pilot, Will Adams, a native of Gillingham, Kent. When Adams stepped thankfully ashore he became the first Englishman to enter Japan. Iyeyasu summoned him to his presence, liked him and persuaded Adams to stay in Japan and teach him all he could about European conditions, mathematics, navigation, maritime lore

and other subjects and then to supervise the building of a ship in the European style.

In return for his services, Iyeyasu gave Will Adams an estate and showed him many favours, employing him also as a diplomatic agent when Dutch and English traders arrived in Japan in 1609 and 1613 respectively. Adams, known to the Japanese as Miura Anjin, married a Japanese woman and lived in a house in Yedo in a street named Anjin-cho (Pilot Street) after him. The house stood until 1923. The Kurofune ('Black Ship') shrine to his memory was erected on its site.

At the same time as Iyeyasu was absorbing Adams's teaching he was furthering his own scheme to become ruler. In a battle with his rivals his forces won decisively, largely because the wily Iyeyasu had arranged for a large part of the enemy force to change sides at a critical stage of the fighting. He established himself as Shogun in 1603, abdicated two years later in favour of his son, Hidetada, but stayed on to rule from behind the throne. By 1616 the supporters of the young Hideyori were crushed by Iyeyasu, the boy and his mother driven to suicide in the great castle at Osaka.

The Jesuits, jealous of Iyeyasu's favour denounced Will Adams as a pirate; but he, showing greater Christianity offered them whatever help he could give. Iyeyasu observed this and noted that the Western world was by no means united under Christianity nor Christianity within itself. His doubts about it deepened, especially when he began to hear stories of the corruption of Japanese officials by cunning European traders. A survey of the coast was being made by a Spanish mariner. He had permission but Adams hinted to his master that it might be another prelude to an attempted take-over Iyeyasu followed Hideyoshi's example and issued anti-Christian edicts. They were not enforced at once for fear of disrupting profitable trade. But in 1614 he ordered the expulsion of all foreign priests from 'the country of the gods and of Buddha'. When Iyeyasu died in 1616 his son Hidetada began many years of persecution of Christians, both converts and foreign missionaries and priests. Some priests had remained sheltered by their converts. Others had gone but secretly returned. Now it was made a capital offence to be a Christian. Jesuits, friars and their following were tortured to make them repudiate their faith. Many of them refused and died horribly. The biggest blow to Christianity in Japan fell in 1637 when the strongly Christian community of a district of Kyushu rebelled against the oppressive measures of two local daimyo. Some 37,000 men, women and children fortified themselves in an old castle and its grounds at Hara, where they endured a seige which they must have known held no hope for them. Their numbers decimated, they withdrew at last to Shimoshima, largest of the offshore Amakusa Islands, and made their last stand. After enduring three months seige by forces sent by the Shogun and bombardment at one time by a Dutch vessel they were overcome and massacred almost to the last person. Shimoshima today treasures many relics of the martyrdom and Japanese schoolchildren are taught respect for the Christians who died rather than renounce their faith.

The slaughter nearly marked the end of Christianity, but like Catholics in Cromwell's England in that same century Christians in Japan were winkled out one by one and liquidated: yet, like the Catholics, they found ways of keeping their creed secretly alive.

Right: Tokugawa family crest
Below: Sakitsu Church,
Amakusa Islands

41

Many of the Christian slogans on the martyrs' banners had been in Portuguese, and the Shogun strongly suspected that nation of having engineered the Shimabara uprising. He expelled all Portuguese and Spanish traders. The English had already left voluntarily after their trading post had failed. The Dutch were allowed to stay, though confined to the island of Deshima in Nagasaki harbour. Japanese were forbidden to

Foreign merchant

On the Tokaido Road. From a wood-block by Hiroshige

leave the country. Having found contact with the West brought more trouble than advantages, the Japanese were making the first of their bids for isolation.

The Tokugawa family, determined to remain in control for ever, took steps to deter any form of rebellion. Territories were again realigned, so that faithful followers could keep an eye on their neighbours. The Shogunate, now based on Yedo, made every daimyo waste part of his time at court, engaging in pointless ceremonial, so that there was little chance for plotting. Returning to his estates, the daimyo had to leave his wife and family in Yedo as hostages.

The constant coming and going to Yedo brought into prominence the Tokaido, or grand trunk road, from Kyoto to Yedo (brilliantly depicted by the wood-block artist Hiroshige). Every day saw a bustle on it of pilgrims, priests, merchants, messengers and the glittering cavalcades of the daimyos, with their servants and superbly decorated waggons carrying gifts to the court, guarded by samurai with their two swords.

Japan was now a police state. Along the trunk roads were many checkpoints where spies scrutinized all who passed and pried into their belongings, fearful of arms being smuggled into the capital for an uprising. The death penalty was imposed for trying to avoid these barriers. The idea was to make travelling as difficult as possible for all but the closely watched daimyos, so that the populace would stay at home, and keep out of mischief. The system worked. It put a virtual end to clan warfare throughout the country and, with the ending of outside contact, gave Japan an enviable 250 years of peace. Yet she missed much by her isolation, for those years were ones of great change and progress in the West from which Japan would have benefited.

One of several artistic forms brought to perfection at this time was the Bunraku puppet drama, a form of theatre unique

to Japan. It comprises historical and domestic dramas acted
entirely by elaborate puppets, half life-size (*left* and *above*).
Each requires three highly trained operators – a chief manipulator and two assistants, all of whom wear self-effacing black
garments and remain silent and quite expressionless throughout
the performance. Working as one man, with fantastic skill,
though in full view of the audience, they can produce remarkably naturalistic performances which make one forget that one

is watching puppets. It is not widespread in Japan today but a company has performed in America, Britain and other parts of the West in recent years with great acclaim.

The chief manipulator holds the puppet upright and operates an inner control with cords to move the eyes, eyebrows and mouth. His right hand moves its right arm. One assistant manages the left arm and the third the feet. Samisen players point the drama or pathos of the action; but the highest-ranked performer is the narrator who recites the story. His exacting duty is to provide different voices for anything up to seven characters of all ages and both sexes, addressing one another. All concerned with Bunraku need many years of training and are dedicated to the art.

Bunraku puppets have been regarded so seriously that some of their plays have been written by Japan's leading play-

Merchant, samurai and peasant

Scene from a kabuki play

wrights, including Chikamatsu Monzaemon (1653–1724), 'the Japanese Shakespeare'. Such plays were also adopted by a further form of theatre, Kabuki, stemming from both Bunraku and Noh. It attained its present form in the late seventeenth century after women had been banned from the Japanese stage. Since then, women's roles have been played very skilfully by men. Kabuki embodies historical, domestic and dance dramas, with the accent upon beauty of colour and poise, performed to the music of a small ensemble.

One of the most famous Bunraku and Kabuki plays is the Chusingura – 'Forty-seven Ronin'. In 1703, two daimyo, Lord Asano and Lord Kira, arrived in Yedo. They quarrelled and Kira insulted Asano, who drew his dagger and wounded him. It was a capital offence to draw a weapon at court and Asano was obliged to commit seppuku, or hara-kiri. His forty-seven followers, now ronin, or masterless warriors, swore revenge on Kira. One snowy night they entered his mansion and requested him to commit seppuku. When he refused, they cut off his head and laid it on Asano's tomb. All of them committed seppuku and were buried side by side. Homage is still paid to them by throngs of visitors and a memorial service is held every 14 December.

To commit seppuku or hara-kiri (literally 'belly-cut') a man would don a white robe and kneel before the family shrine. After praying he would thrust a knife into his belly and draw it across and then up. If he faltered a waiting friend would behead him.

Music developed in step with the theatre. The samisen,

Kira wounded by Asano

48

The ronin storm Kira's house

49

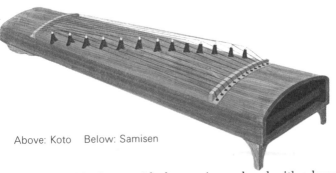

Above: Koto   Below: Samisen

a balalaika-like banjo with three strings, played with a large ivory plectrum, became the standard accompaniment to narrative singing in the puppet houses and found its way into the spreading entertainment districts of Yedo. The koto, a horizontal harp with thirteen strings, developed from the ancient court zither, was adopted in private homes. The simple bamboo recorder became the subtle shakuhachi, much favoured by wandering priests. Other traditional instruments of Japan include the biwa, a four-stringed mandolin picked with the fingers, and the sho, a kind of Pan-pipes.

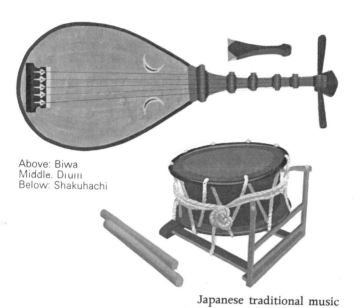

Above: Biwa
Middle: Drum
Below: Shakuhachi

Japanese traditional music is full of subtleties not easily accessible to the Western ear. Emphasis tends to be upon the beat, rather than the tune, and the sound strikes us as scratchy, high-pitched, wailing and lacking in rich textures. Yet Japanese folk songs, bellowed lustily at festivals, and many of the lullabies and play songs of children are instantly likeable. For their part the Japanese have never found much trouble in appreciating Western music. Excellent orchestras and soloists draw packed and discerning audiences in fine concert halls, and far more Japanese children study Western instruments than their own.

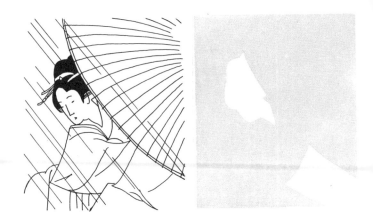

Japan's most original art is the type of wood-block print known as ukiyoye – pictures of the fleeting world, the passing everyday pleasures. Japan's tradition of printing goes back to the eleventh century but the Tokugawa period saw a remarkable flowering after the copper-plate printing introduced from the West had been discredited along with the Christianity it had helped to propagate. Living in a dour, samurai-dominated time, the eighteenth-century Japanese were delighted to buy – for practically nothing – the ukiyoye prints of actors, courtesans, geishas and other people and places associated with wordly pleasures which were produced by a school of artists with brilliant instinct for line and colour. Original paintings were too expensive for ordinary folk. Wood engravings, from which pictures could be mass-produced, were the perfect substitute.

A picture is drawn on paper, then pasted face downward on a block of cherry wood. The details of the design are traced into the wood with knives and other tools, then ink or paint is applied with a soft brush and the block pressed by hand on to paper; or else numerous sectional blocks are used one at a time – as many as fourteen to one print – each representing part of the picture and painted with its own colour, delicately shaded, and applied in perfect register to produce a marvellous whole, such as 'Rainstorm at Shono' by Hiroshige (1797–1858), from his series 'Fifty-three stations of the Tokaido'.

The two haiku by Basho,
penned and illustrated
by the poet

Ukiyoye prints by the greatest masters are sought all over the world today and change hands for thousands of dollars or hundreds of pounds but there are countless imitations and a great number of fakes; so, buyer, beware! The style, with its concentration upon design, economy of line and subtlety of suggestion, rather than the realistic representation of subjects, has influenced many Western artists, notably Whistler. The ukiyoye artists were often of comparatively low birth and standing, which perhaps accounts for their ability to hit upon subjects immensely to the taste of the general public of their time. But a masterly print owes its perfection not only to a

Hokusai (1760–1849) was one of the greatest landscape artists. Below is his 'Mount Fuji from Kanagawa', from his fine series of views of the peerless mountain near Yedo. Landscape was widely popular amongst a public whose travelling was so restricted.

Utamaro (1754–1805) excelled all others in his pictures of beautiful women, but was also a master at depicting flowers, birds and insects. Above is a detail from his 'Kitchen Scene'.

great artist but to the dextrous engraver, whose knife and chisel reproduced the design in wood, and to the printer responsible for making the repeated applications of the block, coated with delicate colours made from vegetable dyes, on to the paper, pressing it by hand and achieving exact register every time.

Japanese prints can be found in many museums and galleries in the West, notably in London, Boston and New York.

A considerable literary revival belongs also to the time of the Tokugawas. It started in the late seventeenth century, when the plays of Chikamatsu and the novels of Saikaku reached out for the first time to a public beyond the refined court circle: but its best-known manifestation, one which has had a recent resurgence in the West, is the haiku (pronounced 'hike') poem.

Poetry has always been a popular form of expression in Japan, which derived it, like many other things, from China. During the cultural blossoming which attended the eleventh century Heian period, a pastime grew among the languid court folk of composing waka, thirty-one-syllable poems of five lines – 5, 7, 5, 7, 7 syllables. Poetry parties would be held at which guests would cap one another's verses.

The haiku springs from this and achieves the same sort of results with greater economy. It has three lines of five, seven and five syllables respectively, which allows a total of no more than ten words. It has neither metre nor rhyme and must embody a reference to one of the seasons. The uninitiated would not recognize a reference to violets, willows or un-melted snow as implying spring; 'the moon' automatically meaning the harvest moon, therefore autumn; and so on. As in all Japan's arts the rules are intricate and the discipline they impose has helped keep formlessness, obscurity and degeneration at bay.

The most celebrated of haijin, as the haiku poets are known, was Basho (1644–94) who renounced the samurai's calling to live as a poor pilgrim poet student of Buddhism and master of many disciples. On the opposite page are his two most famous haiku.

Kare-eda ni
Karasu no tomari keri
Aki no kure.

A solitary crow
Upon a leafless bough
One Autumn eve.

Furuike ya
Kawazu tobikomu
Mizu no oto.

The ancient pond –
A frog has plunged:
Splash!

(Frog is one of the words symbolizing spring.)

The two haiku by Basho, penned and illustrated by the poet. The brief haiku relies upon precise choice of words to evoke image and atmosphere and so much that has to be left unsaid must be implied. In terms of painting the haiku is like a sketch that says all it needs to say without the need of elaborate detail. So Basho's simple illustrations, emphasizing only one or two features, exactly match the content of his poems.

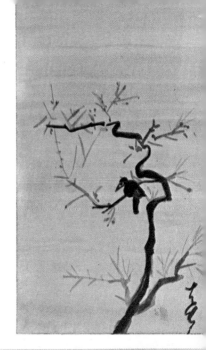

Odd verse one might think. But haiku contemplated at length and in a receptive frame of mind, can evoke atmosphere strangely and conjure to the eye the sort of scene depicted with such economy of brush-stroke in Japanese paintings. Seemingly artless, they are full of art and difficult to compose well.

FORCED BACK INTO THE WORLD

Denied contact with the outside world, intelligent Japanese stirred uneasily under a dictatorial rule. Russian, British and American ships risked putting into Japanese ports for supplies and hoping to do some trading. Some crews were massacred. Others were ordered to leave at once. After protests the Japanese agreed that ships in distress might water and fuel in their ports. But in 1839 when Congress sent Commodore Biddle to try to negotiate a trade agreement, he was jostled by an ordinary Japanese seaman. Under strict orders to keep the peace, he failed to demand the man's punishment. To the Japanese this spelled weakness. They contemptuously refused Congress's request.

Britain or Russia seemed closest to opening up Japan. Britain's earlier attempts to trade there had been unsuccessful; but following the Opium War of 1842, Hong Kong was a

Commodore Biddle

Left:
Japanese
shore battery
firing at an
American ship

British port and her ships were often in Japanese waters.

As early as 1805 Russia had had a vessel lying off Nagasaki, on board an official envoy vainly waiting to be invited ashore. Now, with the colonization of Siberia proceeding, she needed some nearby source of supplies and looked again to Japan.

But America's Far Eastern ambitions were even more urgent. Her trade with China, through the port of Canton, was developing rapidly and many of her finest ships were using the Great Circle route. This was the shortest way to China from the U.S.A., and took them close to Japan, a more promising source from where to replenish the supplies which the new steamers, especially, needed. Enterprising Americans wanted a foothold in Japan, so that they might become the principal traders both there and in China.

In October 1852 the Russian Admiral Putyatin sailed with four ships for Japan, empowered to demand a trade treaty. He got to Nagasaki in August 1853 a few weeks too late. Another fleet of four ships had reached Japan in July. Its commander was Commodore Matthew Perry, U.S. Navy.

Commodore Perry

Commodore Perry had lived for nearly sixty years and had served the U.S. Navy for almost forty-five of them. He was shrewd, tough and autocratic. Whereas the unfortunate Biddle had been forbidden to deal firmly with the Japanese, Perry had been promised an extraordinarily free hand, his instructions hinting that any indiscretion he might find it politic to commit would be 'viewed with indulgence' by his President. He knew that even his limited fleet could cut off the bulk of Yedo's food supplies, which reached it by sea, and play havoc with fishing boats. The more realistic Japanese recognized this, too, and knew that America could easily impose her demands on them by force. This possibility, in fact, was not absent from Perry's own mind. He suggested to his government that if the Japanese should turn down his demands the Pacific island of Okinawa should be annexed as a base for military operations against them.

Perry's squadron sailed bodly into Uraga, the scene of Biddle's humiliation. Perry refused to discuss his business with minor officials sent to sidetrack him. He handed over a letter from President Fillimore requesting a trade treaty and guaranteed supplies for shipping, distributed some mechanical toys and other small gifts; then, declaring that he would be

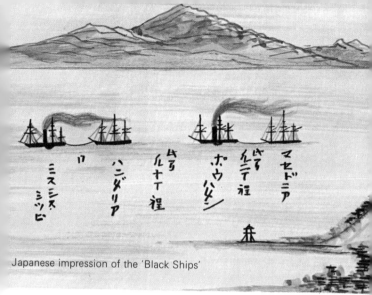

ミスシスシッピ　ハニダリア　ルヿ十丁程　ホウハ丿ゝ　仝テ仝程　マセドニア

Japanese impression of the 'Black Ships'

back in the spring, sailed away. He pointedly let the people of Yedo get a good view of his formidable ships – two steamers and two sailing vessels, with nearly 600 men. This display of courteous firmness impressed the Japanese, though their chief reaction was of alarm. The arrival soon afterwards of Putyatin's ships made plain the West's determination not to be put off any longer. Undecided what to do, the Shogunate asked all daimyos for their comments.

Some daimyos, ignoring Japan's lack of a navy or any coastal defences, were all for driving off the outsiders. More realistic ones counselled opening up trade, with the idea that Japan should learn all she could from the foreigners and turn it to her own advantage. The Shogunate decided upon a typically Japanese compromise. The Americans would not be rebuffed, yet they would be given no firm answer to their demands. At the same time, defences would be prepared and troops trained. The shores of Yedo Bay began to seethe with the drilling of men and the building of gun positions. But when Perry hove into sight again, in February 1854, this time with seven ships and 2,000 men, the Shogunate must have known that its bluff was about to be called, and that no defences would hold the Americans for long.

61

Foreigners in Japan — a Japanese view

Using an occasional judicial threat, Perry quickly got the Treaty of Kanagawa signed at Yokohama on 31 March 1854. It agreed that the ports of Hakodate and Shimoda be opened for American ships to trade and get supplies. Shipwrecked sailors would be helped and protected, and an American consul stationed at Shimoda. The first holder of this office arrived in 1856. Townsend Harris was a man with Perry's blend of strength and resolution, qualities admired by the Japanese. Against much resistance he obtained an audience with the Shogun at Yedo. The Shogun was impressed. He vowed never-ending relations with the West.

Perry's negotiations lasted six weeks and gave the West a new word – tycoon. Though we associate it with big business, its original form, taikun, means 'great prince'. It had been hastily adopted by the Shogun to impress the Western negotiators, since 'Shogun' alone meant merely Generalissimo, not nearly grand enough. Perry was not a man to be overawed by a title. His job done, he sailed away to China. Although it had taken a grander name the Shogunate had come closer to losing power. In the eyes of the Japanese people it had allowed the barbarian to enter their land. The cry 'Sonno Joi' – 'Revere the Sovereign: expel the barbarians' – began to be heard. One morning in 1860, Ii Naosuke, an important counsellor who had taken it on ·himself to sanction treaties giving further concessions to American, British, Russian and French interests, was set upon and killed by samurai, who then committed hara-kiri. Hurriedly, the Tokugawas married off the young Shogun to the Emperor's sister, so as to tie themselves firmly to the royal line.

Some Japanese held the opinion that a change in their national way of life had been long overdue. As world communications improved rapidly it was no longer realistic for any nation to try to live in self-contained isolation. But many more people felt understandably shocked and affronted that their government should have given way to the first clear threats to be uttered against the country by a foreign power.

Townsend Harris received by the shogun

63

The United States consul, Townsend Harris, gained many concessions for his country, at the same time working skilfully on Japanese fears of what Britain, the mightiest power in the East, might intend. Britain, represented by an able figure, Sir Harry Parkes, favoured imperial rule and would have been glad to see the country unified under the Emperor. France's capable minister, Léon Roches, worked equally energetically to assure the Shogunate that its rule was what his country preferred, and the rumour got about that a secret treaty had been signed by the two countries. Those Japanese onlookers who were close enough to the seats of power to see these diplomatic manoeuvres going on began to be disturbed at the growing extent of foreign influence.

Inevitably, a number of resentful acts occurred, including beatings of foreigners, robbery and even murder. Early instances of the latter were the killing of two guards at the British Legation in Yedo and the cutting down from his horse by two swordsmen of an Englishman named Richardson as he travelled the Tokaido Road in September 1862. More peaceably, the Emperor had made up his mind to get rid of the foreigners by expulsion and issued orders to that effect to the Shogunate. In passing them on the Shogunate officials added their own assurance to the diplomats that they would not be carried out. But in June 1863 shore batteries of the rising Choshu clan opened fire on foreign vessels in the Shimonoseki Straits. American and French warships retaliated vigorously, but a British squadron took the firmest measure. In retaliation against the Satsuma clan, whom it held responsible for the murder of Richardson, a British squadron bombarded the town of Kagoshima, reducing it to rubble, though with little loss of life. This stern reprisal, far from leaving a legacy of resentment, earned the respect of the Japanese and led to a long friendship between Britain and Japan and especially between their navies. In September 1864 a combined British, American, Dutch and French fleet bombarded Shimonoseki and destroyed the shore batteries, before demanding an indemnity of three million dollars for hostile acts. It had been made abundantly clear that the barbarians were determined to have their own way.

Murder of Richardson

The bombardments had been not so much against Japan as directed at the Choshu clan, whose aggressive attitude, well-drilled troops and modern equipment had made it too strong even for the Shogunate to handle. Kagoshima had been the capital of another belligerent clan, the Satsuma. Once rivals but now allies, the clans pledged themselves to restore the ancient character of their country by ridding it of foreigners, doing away with Shoguns and restoring imperial rule. The Shogun, blamed for the damage suffered in the bombardments, tried to discipline them but they were too powerful.

Shogunate forces march to attack the daimyo of Choshu

In 1866 the twenty-year-old Shogun died childless and was succeeded reluctantly by the intelligent Keiki, who was already convinced that Japan could not live on in isolation. Early next year the Emperor Komei died and was succeeded by his fifteen-year-old son Mutsuhito, who adopted the significant title of Meiji – 'Enlightened Government'. Influential clan headsmen at once approached Keiki to restore true rule to the Emperor. He agreed readily. So, a system of dual rule which had lasted 350 years came to an end and Japan was ready to move forward in the world context and start a new phase in her development.

Five young Choshu samurai had secretly visited Europe, intending to learn to their advantage from scientific achievement there and had been impressed by what they had seen of a mercantile and industrial might that must eventually prove irresistible. They returned home to beg their people to call off their futile resistance to the West. Many Japanese shared this view. The Choshu, Satsuma and other powerful clans pointed the way by instituting modernizing reforms; but the Tokugawa family, in whose hands the Shogunate had been for so long, were not going to give in without a protest. They rebelled at several places and held out bravely for some months. Isolated incidents against foreigners continued to occur. The British consul, Sir Harry Parkes, and his entourage were attacked by two fanatical samurai on the way to his first audience with the Emperor. A Japanese attendant cut one down and Lord Redesdale overpowered another. The Emperor stated his official attitude towards the West in his Charter Oath: 'Knowledge shall be sought over all the world and thus shall be strengthened the foundation of the imperial policy.' In modern idiom, 'If you can't beat them, join them; and then perhaps you can beat them later'.

The Meiji Period (1867–1912) has been termed Japan's Victorian Age, and there are many similarities. Meiji himself is revered as one of the world's most enlightened sovereigns. He began as he meant to go on by breaking well-established precedents. He let it be known to foreign officials that his name should be substituted for the Shogun's in existing treaties, and that new negotiations should be conducted with him as head of state. He invited foreign diplomatists to his court, even showed himself in public, and promised all classes a say in government, with administration and laws based on justice instead of ancient custom and privilege. He moved his court in the autumn of 1868 from Kyoto to Yedo, which he renamed Tokyo – 'Eastern Capital' – and made an Imperial Palace of the former Shogun's fortress. As the divine ruler passed along the ancient Tokaido Road, part of his progress was marked by the playing of 'The British Grenadiers' by a British military band. When the Meiji Period ended (1912) Japan was a world power.

Imperial Palace, Tokyo

The entry of the Western nations into Japan brought her certain risks. She had no national army, next to no navy; she was economically and industrially backward. The domination which had been feared ever since the days of the Jesuits and Dominicans could have been brought about. But the incoming flow of Westerners was more a trickle than a flood. The Japanese welcomed them. Perhaps because of their long isolation, the Japanese people have a well-developed sense of curiosity and they found plenty to study in the remarkable ways of the West. There was soon a craze for Japanese versions of Western dress and ladies' hairstyles.

However, there were more important introductions: a central system of taxation, banks, lighthouses, docks, telegraph offices. The first railway between Tokyo and Yokohama opened in 1872. The following year the Gregorian calendar and the seven-day week were introduced. Elementary education was made compulsory, an imperial army was formed and was trained by French officers, a British-pattern navy placed under British instructors. Foreigners were found in such posts as engineers, legal advisers, coastal pilots and teachers, while Japanese went to study in such countries as France and England.

Japanese versions of Victorian European dress

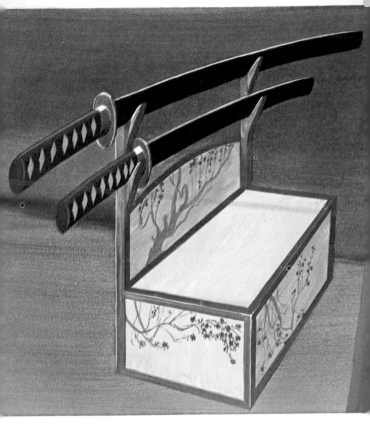

A samurai's laid-up swords

Internal government was remodelled on a system of local prefectures. As a peace-keeping move, only policemen and regular soldiers and sailors were permitted swords. This dealt a crushing blow to the warrior class, for now any humbly-born military conscript could carry a sword while a samurai, with centuries of family tradition, could not. Forbidden also to wear the traditional top-knot of hair, the samurai were further humiliated with small pensions and petty appointments, though some who swallowed their pride and entered the despised merchant class found prosperity. But out of two million of them – in a population of thirty-three millions – perhaps a quarter were left without means of support.

Inevitably, a rebellion began to grow, and where there is incipient revolt a leader is soon thrust up. His name was Saigo Takamori – literally, the great Saigo. Big in body and mind, Saigo was just the man for the role. He was important in the government and a leader of a move to invade Korea. Outvoted by moderates who could see that a Korean campaign would conflict with Russia's Asian designs, he resigned and went to his home province of Satsuma to set up military academies to teach old techniques and traditions of warfare. Discontented samurai flocked to him and in 1877 he led 40,000 of them into several months of rebellion, scrupulously aimed not at the Emperor but at his allegedly corrupt and inefficient advisers. His campaign ended in a bloody battle near Kagoshima, against a government conscript army. Clearly losing, Saigo asked a friend to behead him, which most of his closest followers emulated by committing harakiri. The conscripts' victory had shown that any ordinary Japanese could fight as well as a samurai, from which it was inferred that all Japanese could rise supreme in arms over anyone.

Saigo and his dog – statue in Ueno Park, Tokyo

The year 1890 was significant for Japan. After several years in the making a new constitution was proclaimed by Emperor Meiji. The constitution gave freedom of expression and association, immunity from invasion of privacy and freedom of religious belief. It carefully embodied a clause under which these rights might be suspended in national emergency in the interests of law, thereby rendering them virtually meaningless.

The Rescript on Education was also published in 1890, requiring a copy of itself, with portraits of the Emperor and his consort, to be kept in every school and read out by the headmaster with grave ceremony on national commemoration days. The Rescript assumed almost sacred proportions in children's minds, with the result that in adulthood each would offer himself unhesitatingly and courageously to the state when called on to do so.

The new patriotism brought some decline in the fashion for aping foreign ways. All the same a big hall, the Rokumeikan (*below*), designed by a British architect, was erected in Tokyo especially to house social gatherings of Japanese and foreigners. Japanese ladies in bustles danced with Westerners or learnt cookery and music from European ladies.

But the clan which had crushed Saigo's rebellion – the Sat-Cho, a clique of the Satsuma and Choshu – was now powerfully placed in control of the army, navy, finance, industry, civil service and education. The new constitution made the public aware of this and caused unrest, both in and out of parliament. Then in 1894 Japan suddenly went to war with China and unrest at home ended abruptly.

Right: A teacher displays the Rescript on Education

RISE OF THE MILITARISTS

Japan attacked China in July 1894 without any formal declaration of war and achieved striking surprise success – a lesson not to be forgotten. She advanced rapidly across the Chinese frontier, taking Port Arthur, the only part of the Manchurian coastline that is always ice-free. With her very heart and capital threatened, China asked for peace. Terms were agreed that would give Japan control of Formosa, the Pescadores and the whole of the Liaotung Peninsula, including Port Arthur.

Alarmed by this shift of balance in the East, Russia, France and Germany, in the 'Triple Intervention', 'suggested' that Japan give up her Manchurian gains. Emperor Meiji managed to persuade his people to accept this appalling loss of face. It meant the end of respect for the Western world. The crowning insult came in 1900, when Russia moved into occupation of the Liaotung Peninsula and Port Arthur, from where she had been largely instrumental in expelling Japan.

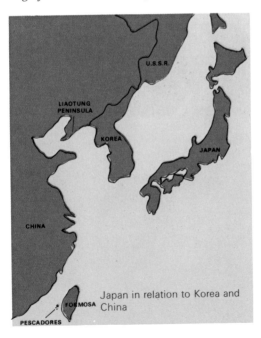

Japan in relation to Korea and China

Japanese artillery in action

Russia's presence in Manchuria seemed to present a real menace. She was developing the Trans-Siberian railway to Port Arthur, giving her a supply route which pointed to a take-over of Korea. Japan was glad to make a treaty which committed Britain to come to her aid if more than one Western power should attack her. She now felt confident enough to exert pressure on Russia to leave Manchuria. But over five months of talks achieved nothing. On 6 February 1904 Japan broke off negotiations. Within two days her troops had occupied the

Korean capital, Seoul. Destroyers and torpedo boats under Vice-Admiral Togo arrived at Port Arthur by night to find the Russian fleet at anchor. Torpedoes struck several ships almost simultaneously. The Japanese declared war the next day. Most Britons felt warmly towards their ally, whose navy had been largely built in their shipyards and trained by Royal Naval officers. Japan's justification for striking a surprise blow was that at the other end of the Trans-Siberian railway lay the whole might of Russia.

The Russian fleet tries to escape from Port Arthur

The Russo-Japanese War was short – some eighteen months – and spectacular. It was the biggest modern war yet seen, with large, clear-cut battles and many casualties, yet with both sides displaying such old-fashioned virtues as chivalry, humanity and great bravery. Fortunately for Japan, Russia did not throw in the huge forces she might have done; yet the world saw the war in terms of a gallant little nation standing up to a tyrannous big one, and beating it.

The best-remembered land battle of the war was the siege of Port Arthur to where the Russian commander on that front, General Stessel, withdrew his forces in October 1904. Their position was a powerful one. Port Arthur was heavily fortified, its main positions surrounded by formidable moats in which were sown mines which could be detonated electrically as attackers tried to pass over them. Barbed wire entanglements, sharp spikes and other hazards had been prepared and the defenders, in bomb-proof steel shelters, had removed heavy guns from warships to add to their already impressive fire-power. The Japanese at first tried direct assault on this powerful stronghold and paid dearly for their rashness; but after five months' siege in which they learned a lot about modern warfare and applied it with patience, they proved triumphant, although the effort had cost them some 60,000 casualties.

With Port Arthur in their hands they could turn their confident attention to another front. In the frozen February of 1905 they initiated what was to be a three-weeks battle against General Kuropatkin's strong forces at Mukden. Nearly three-quarters of a million men of both sides were involved, and the decisive Japanese victory ended with something like one-fifth of that total killed or wounded. The Japanese generals became world famous, especially Nogi, who had captured Port Arthur and Oyama, who had gained the ultimate victory at Mukden. Unluckily for them, Japan had concentrated on training and equipping her front-line army at the expense of her reserves. With such big losses in hard-fought battles there were not enough supporting troops for the generals to use to consolidate and follow up their gains, or the Russians would have been thoroughly routed. As it was the outcome was disastrous for Russia and was one of the chief immediate causes of the Russian Revolution of 1905.

Above: Manchuria. Port Arthur is at the tip of the Liaotung Peninsula where the Trans-Siberian railway terminates. China is at top left, Korea bottom right.
Below: Japanese troops celebrate their resounding victory in the Russo-Japanese war. The decisive success in a modern war of their small, new army and navy over one of the world's greatest powers gave the Japanese confidence and ambition to become strong and influential amongst nations; but the material rewards of victory were derisory, leading to a legacy of bitterness against Western interference.

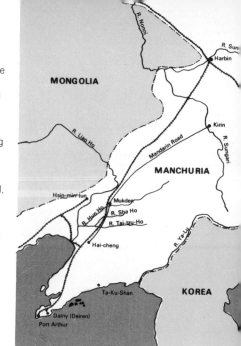

Russian ships sunk at Port Arthur

The Japanese Navy, too, threw up a hero to capture the world's imagination. Vice-Admiral Togo scored an immense victory which virtually brought the Russo-Japanese War to an end. Having, after a long wait, brought the Russian Port Arthur squadron into action, destroyed part of it and put the rest to flight, Togo prudently took his ships back to Japan for a complete refit. While this was being done, Russia's only remaining fleet, the Baltic Fleet, was making a remarkable passage from its home base to join in the campaign. It was a vast armada, ranging from ageing battleships and swift destroyers to plodding colliers and store-ships, whose route lay all the way round the Cape, India and Malaya. Having nearly provoked Britain to enter the war by mistaking British trawlers for Japanese torpedo boats, and firing on them, the fleet at length reached Japanese waters. The voyage had taken over half a year, so that the vessels' manoeuvrability had become hampered by thick marine growths on their bottoms, while the sailors were understandably jaded. As the fresh though nervous Japanese fleet prepared to do battle, Togo deduced that the Russian Admiral Rozhestvenski would head for Vladivostock and a refit via the Tshushima Strait between Kyushu and Korea. He was right. The two fleets met in the strait and within two days the Russian armada, after sailing half-way round the world to get there, was almost wholly sunk or captured.

Battle of Mukden

Japan had won the biggest modern war, using modern weapons and tactics against one of the world's mightiest powers. Yet with Russia's naval strength destroyed and her land forces in Manchuria routed, it was Japan who sought peace. America's President Theodore Roosevelt was asked to mediate and agreed at once. To the astonishment and indignation of the jubilant Japanese the terms their country demanded were derisorily mild. All Japan got was Russian recognition of Japan's interest in Korea, the lease of the Liaotung Peninsula and the southern section of the Manchurian railway, and the southern half of the island of Sakhalin. Both countries agreed to withdraw their forces from Manchuria. Japan asked for a cash indemnity of some eight million pounds but Russia refused to pay.

When the Japanese public learned this pathetic reward for their army and navy's brilliant victories there were riots of protest. Martial law had to be declared. The truth the public had not known was that their country had run out of money and resources. Victory had come almost too late. Japan had neither the strength to fight on further or to impose her will on the peace conference, and had meekly to accept what the mediators recommended and the Russians consented to concede.

But there were invisible gains. Japan was now an international power to be reckoned with. It was a great feat of arms and a major boost to her reputation that she had achieved such a victory less than forty years after emerging from semi-feudal isolation, and had influenced world events by turning Russia's interest back from the East to Europe, with consequences which would help to bring about the First World War. It was a tribute to Japan's adaptability, her genius for learning from others and employing their ways, and not least to the qualities of her warriors who had fought not only bravely but with discipline and restraint in victory.

It was in the minds of many who showed greatest discontent at the outcome of the war that Japan might have elected herself leader of an all-Asian bloc embracing China, India and smaller countries. Extreme nationalist groups dedicated to this sort of cause sprang up and menaced society under such names as the Black Dragon Society. They used bribery, blackmail and violence to make their points and infiltrated the armed forces.

Admiral Togo

At the same time there was a surge of Socialist feeling. The red flag and the dogma of Socialism became familiar in Japan. They survived official suppression until 1911, when the police announced the discovery of a plot to murder the Emperor. This was too much for the ordinary Japanese, who could accept the murder of prime ministers as a political necessity but never that of the divine ruler. Socialism was thus effectively wiped out by sheer unpopularity.

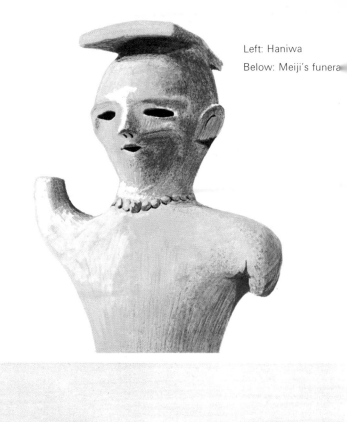

Left: Haniwa

Below: Meiji's funera

In 1912 the Emperor Meiji died after a reign of forty-five years. His era had seen the opening of the country to the world, her amazing progress, her newly-acquired stature not merely as a power in Asia – the Emperor disliked the expression – but among all nations. He was deeply mourned. His impressive night-time funeral procession was watched by huge crowds and included a detachment of Royal Marines from the British flagship in the Far East. He was buried near Kyoto. Of his many memorials the Meiji Shrine in Tokyo is the most impressive. But though he symbolized modernity, the revival of an ancient custom attended his death. In early times when an Emperor was entombed his retainers were buried alive up to the neck nearby, until they perished and were able to escort him to the other world. In time this became regarded as barbarous, so clay effigies, known as haniwa (*left*), were buried instead. As many as 10,000 have been recovered from one 1,600 year old burial mound. After the Emperor died in 1912, four earthen effigies of armoured warriors were buried with him, and General Nogi, hero of Port Arthur, committed seppuku in order to accompany his Emperor. To Western eyes Japan proved that she was still not fully of the modern world.

Meiji's successor, Yoshihito, took the name Taisho, 'Great Righteousness'. He was a sickly man who held no promise of his great father's qualities. Japan herself was in sickly state. The war had drained her resources and disenchanted much of her population. Her birth-rate was higher than ever before – the population numbered about fifty million in 1910 – straining food production to the limit. Even such basic food as rice was being imported, so that her balance of payments was unfavourable. There was political unrest and an uneasy feeling that all was not well at the top, with the Sat-Cho still very much in control and chief government posts going automatically to

Japanese shipyards building warships

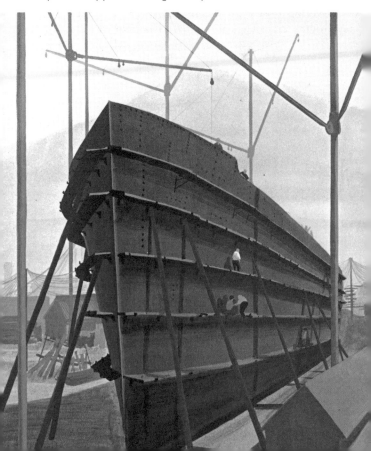

generals and admirals. Despite her newly-acquired international prestige, Japan was unhappy in her relations with other powers. It took another war to divert her people's minds from these troubles and to restore prosperity overnight.

When the First World War broke out Japan unhesitatingly entered on the Allied side and commenced operations against Germany. Tsingtao, Germany's principal possession in China, was quickly overcome and Japan assumed the administration of the territory. It was a very satisfactory way of getting a foothold in China, though Japan spoilt things by demanding wide powers. She got them but ruined what remained of her relations with that country and disgusted the Western powers. In 1915 Japan presented the Twenty-One Demands to China; they were intended to reduce China to a protectorate, but the other world powers opposed and prevented the execution of the demands which amounted to outright imperialism. Nevertheless the Japanese navy were able to seize the central Pacific islands, the Marshalls, Carolines and Marianas, which Germany had bought from Spain fifteen years before. Her ships did much service to the Royal Navy in helping to escort convoys through the Mediterranean and Indian Oceans and it was partly due to Japanese operations that Admiral von Spee's squadron came to be forced from the western Pacific to the Atlantic, where it was destroyed by the Royal Navy off the Falkland Isles.

Japan's chief help to the Allies was through her factories and shipyards. She could now build the largest warships and her capacity for manufacturing war equipment was becoming enormous. Big Allied orders were filled and the longer the war lasted the more profit Japan made. Her balance of payments soon went from debit to credit, then leaped on to healthy surplus. The zaibatsu, the giant industrial and financial combines, became as wealthy as any in the world. As always in Japan's history the peasants fared worst. Rice riots and strikes occurred with hundreds of deaths. The populace, tired of seeing the existing government party always re-elected, however unpopular its policies or administration, clamoured for electoral reform and achieved its first commoner Prime Minister, Hara. But a movement for universal suffrage got nowhere and the government party was soon back in comfortable control.

In 1917 the Kerensky government in Russia was overthrown by the Bolsheviks. Alarmed at the idea of a Bolshevik regime so close to Manchuria and Korea, and not wishing to miss any advantage arising drom the Western nations' intervention in Russia's civil war, Japan joined the abortive expedition by Britain and the United States to Siberia in 1918. The intervention was unpopular in Japan, whose newly-rich found little profit in it and whose poor saw only further hardship. In any case the downfall of Germany and the triumph of democracy had brought militaristic adventure into discredit.

Having been done down twice at the conference table after successful wars, Japan attended the Peace Conference at Versailles in 1919 resolved to stand up for her rights. She wanted chiefly to stay in the Chinese region of Shantung, which she had taken from the Germans in 1914. The Chinese opposed this, with the sympathy of most other powers; but secret treaties with Britain and France had promised support for Japan, so President Wilson of the U.S.A. could only withdraw his opposition. Possession of Formosa and other islands gave Japan control of the approaches to Japan and north-east Asia. When, at the Washington Conference in 1921, it was agreed

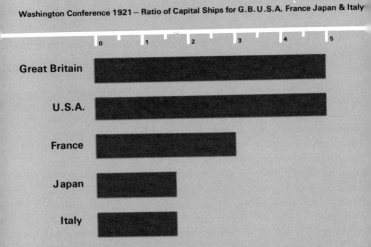

Washington Conference 1921 – Ratio of Capital Ships for G.B. U.S.A. France Japan & Italy

that no new naval bases would be established in the Pacific – referring to the Philippines and Hong Kong – Japan gained added security. At the same time the Naval Treaty laid down that the U.S.A. and Britain should be limited to five major warships for every three held by Japan. As Britain's and America's navies were immeasurably bigger than Japan's already, this meant that while she kept all her navy intact, the others had to scrap many of their ships to get the total down to the required proportions and lay aside plans for building more. Thus, in a paper battle, Japan sank several dozen ships without losing one of her own and emerged an even stronger naval power than before.

The outcome had been successful for Japan, except for one detail. At the Peace Conference she had been elected to a permanent seat in the League of Nations and had asked for a declaration to be inserted in the League Covenant that there should be racial equality between member nations. This had been rejected. For all her satisfactory gains, Japan felt snubbed; and loss of face had always been the hardest thing for her to bear. It rankled, it remained, and it added to her mounting store of bitterness and resentment against the West.

Comparative Power (Naval) in 1924 – G.B. U.S.A. Japan

The numbers shown in this chart do not include ships armed with guns less than 13·5 inch calibre

The Washington Conference also saw the end of the Anglo-Japanese alliance – to the satisfaction of the United States, who had always regarded it as an embarrassment, if not a menace. Japan regretfully signed a virtually meaningless four-power treaty with Britain, the U.S. and France. She signed it with regret. Her ties with Britain had been sincere, based on mutual respect, and now they seemed to be severed. It was ironic that this should have occurred just after the visit to Britain of the twenty-year-old Crown Prince Hirohito, the first time in Japan's history that the heir to the Japanese throne had left her soil. His decision to do so had caused much misgiving at home, and some resentment, but the visit was a distinct success. Hirohito made a popular impression in England through his association with the Prince of Wales, with whom he was seen in golfing clothes to the dismay of older Japanese. Young people were delighted. Western clothing and jazz became the rage. The Prince of Wales returned the visit in 1922. By then the Crown Prince was not only heir to the throne, but Regent, his father having become insane.

Crown Prince Hirohito

Right: Young Japanese couple about to commit suicide by leaping into a volcano

Amongst the gaiety the Japanese budget of 1921 was the heaviest in history. There was a surge of socialist sentiment, but it was badly organized and quickly suppressed by the police. There was confusion in many minds and a rush of suicides. The tradition of hara kiri and its occasional mass use has tended to associate the Japanese with suicide. They do resort to it for reasons which seem trivial to Westerners, though nowadays they favour jumping off bridges, or – especially frustrated young couples – into volcanoes; but the national suicide rate is not as high as in many other countries. The early twenties was a time often now referred to by Japanese as the era of 'Ero, Guro and Nansensu' – Eroticism, Grotesquerie and Nonsense. Suddenly in 1923 a single event sobered everyone and left thousands of carefree young men and girls of Tokyo and Yokohama dead amongst the ashes of their cities.

Devastation after the 1923 Tokyo earthquake

Japan's geographical situation has made her prey from the earliest time to typhoons, tidal waves and earthquakes. There may be up to 2,000 earth tremors in a year, though most can only be detected by instruments. Others last a few seconds and are more alarming than damaging, giving one the sensation of being bodily shaken inside a rattling box or of swaying on the deck of a ship in rough sea, with the attendant seasick feeling. In 1657, when fire followed earthquake and reduced Yedo (Tokyo) to ashes, it is said that 100,000 died. This appalling figure was to be exceeded in an even greater disaster on Saturday morning, 1 September 1923.

It was just before noon and Tokyo and Yokohama offices were about to close for the weekend, when there was a roar like an approaching express train and the earth seemed to lift and then drop with a bone-jarring crash. Tens of thousands of people were trapped or crushed instantly by falling buildings and collapsing roofs. Others rushed into the streets, where they wandered dazedly in great danger as shocks continued and buildings fell about them. The tremors, many of them severe,

continued all afternoon and night but by then little damage was left to be done. Tokyo and Yokohama were mere rubble. Fire had swept through Yokohama, destroying it utterly, and half of Tokyo was also charred ashes. The agony went on for days. Over 1,000 tremors were recorded from 1–5 September.

Anything up to 150,000 people were dead. Billions of yen worth of property had been destroyed, including irreplaceable art treasures and historical records. In the hysteria that followed Koreans and Communists were rumoured to be seizing the chance to overthrow the government. Amidst the chaos many of both were murdered by over-zealous police and patriotic gangs or panic-stricken mobs. It all added up to the biggest natural disaster that has ever been known.

By the 18th the tremors had completely subsided and the Japanese at once started to rebuild their shattered cities. The largely wooden Yedo of old was gone. A modern, sprawling Tokyo arose, together with the efficient new seaport of Yoko-hama. Great Britain, America and China were among those who contributed generously to the disaster fund.

AT ODDS WITH THE WORLD

On Christmas Day 1926 the Emperor Taisho died. He was succeeded by Crown Prince Hirohito and the era of Showa – 'Enlightened Peace' – began. It started well. A democratic parliamentary system was in force for the first time, with votes for all males over twenty-five. The military forces had been cut drastically and the militarists' power seemed to be on the wane. Yet many displaced army officers were giving military instruction in schools and the 'thought police' were active, arresting anyone suspected of 'dangerous thoughts'.

Japan's policy towards the West was moderate, though there was keen resentment over immigration restrictions on Japanese in California and other American states with their implication that the Japanese were a second-class people com-

Both Western and traditional influences can be seen in Tokyo's first skyscraper
Below: A police arrest

pared with Europeans. Japan's relations with China seemed to be improving. The Kuomintang regime under Chiang Kai-shek was at last bringing that disordered country to some semblance of unity and the resentment of the Chinese was directed away from Japan and more towards Britain's presence in their country. But Japanese militarists could see menace in China's becoming unified. Their government's policy towards her was too mild for them. They decided the time was coming to take control into their own hands.

The show-down between the militants and the liberals was provoked by the Prime Minister, Hamaguchi, who, against the urgent advice and pressure of the navy, authorized the signing of the London Naval Treaty of 22 April 1930, whose terms both navy and army saw as a threat to their future. The Japanese delegation at the treaty conference had accepted a ratio of certain warships which seemed less favourable than that agreed for America. The Chief of the Naval Staff objected vehemently. Hamaguchi, a strong-willed man, resisted and convinced his cabinet and the Emperor that the treaty was acceptable. The Privy Council hesitated to ratify it but again Hamaguchi had his way, to the delight of liberal thinkers, who saw a civilian politician refusing to be browbeaten by militarists, although many believed that he had taken too much upon himself. It was known that many in the navy itself supported Hamaguchi; but few people can have been surprised to hear later in the year that Hamaguchi had been shot at Tokyo station. Assassination as a political device was as familiar in Japan as in some Latin countries. Societies formed with high patriotic motives fanned the devotion of their members to fanatic frenzy. Their existence was often known to the police and proved very useful to the army and navy in getting what they wanted by covertly intimidating political opponents who might, like Hamaguchi, have stood up to them. A hint dropped at a meeting that the Emperor's will was being thwarted was enough to inspire some fanatical patriot to assassinate the alleged offender. Although the Emperor had supported Hamaguchi, at least one young man was evidently incensed enough to feel that his country had been put at a disadvantage to the Western signatories of the treaty, and went out with his gun. Hamaguchi was not killed, though critically wounded. He fought back as bravely as ever and tried to return to office within a few months; but he had to resign and was dead in less than a year.

Military officers had been expressly forbidden to take part in politics since the Meiji Restoration so the secret societies served their purpose admirably. Discontent was now growing so rapidly that many officers, especially younger ones, were becoming politically-minded, even to the extent of plotting to seize control of the country. They were spurred on by the economic depression of the 1930's from which Japan suffered like the rest of the world. Hardship was intense amongst soldiers' peasant relatives in many parts of the country. The government seemed to have shrugged off its responsibility to do anything about it. The plain military mind saw that some more authoritarian form of government than free-and-easy democracy was called for. One actual coup was planned to take place in March 1931. It never did but although its details became known to high officials no move was made to punish the culprits. The plotters noted this for future reference.

Socialism again began to rear its head, despite the 'thought police'. Communism as such was abhorrent to the Japanese, but

Shooting of Hamaguchi

they favoured some sort of system whereby the Emperor would control all wealth and share it out in fair proportion. As things stood, the detested capitalists and big business combines had too much of it. Living under harsh discipline, frustrated, longing for activity, the army just had to break out. Events in China gave the army its excuse for action. Something of the sort had been tried on a limited scale in 1928 when the Japanese garrison in south Manchuria had organized the killing of the Chinese war-lord of Manchuria, Chang Tso-lin, by planting a bomb in his railway carriage. The intention had been to spark off a coup to seize Manchuria but it proved abortive. Now another incident occurred in Manchuria involving a bomb and a railway – the blowing up of part of the Pekin–Mukden railway in Japanese-held territory. The 'Mukden Incident' of September 1931 was enough to enable Japanese troops to fire on Chinese and move swiftly to capture the city of Mukden.

Protests flooded in from many countries to the Japanese government. It, too, was protesting – to its own army. It was ignored. Relations between government and army had broken down in the name of 'patriotic' defiance. As the League of Nations called for an end to the fighting and the withdrawal of the troops now spreading all over Manchuria, a dangerous wave of enthusiasm and support for the operations became evident amongst the Japanese people. They too were frustrated and impoverished by the Depression. Manchuria was an old and victorious battle ground for Japan and the fighting gave them the tonic they needed.

Tension between Japan and China over Manchuria had been increasing for some time. The economic and administrative rights acquired by Japan in Manchuria by her victory in the Russo-Japanese war still left formal rule in Chinese hands, which ambitious Japanese now found irksome. For their part, the Chinese resented the continuing Japanese presence on the mainland. When the Chinese wished to build railways in Manchuria, the Japanese objected on the grounds of competition with their own railway system there. Fighting began, and the Japanese government, unable to stop it, was left out on a limb.

China retaliated by boycotting Japanese goods. This proved

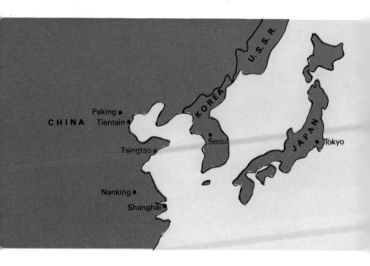

effective so quickly that Japan determined to stop it and landed a small naval force in Shanghai. The Chinese army engaged it and hard fighting ensued, during which the Chinese positions were attacked by Japanese naval planes with an unprecedently savage intensity. Once again the Japanese fighting man demonstrated his toughness and determination. Whether aggressor or defender he could be relied on to fight with almost unparalleled tenacity and seemingly suicidal courage in keeping with the ancient code of bushido, whereby all personal considerations of life and comfort were put aside for blind service to his cause. This was exemplified heroically by three pioneer sappers of a Japanese army force sent in to rescue the hard-pressed naval invaders. When the infantry advance became held up by dense barbed wire, privates Sakue, Kitagawa and Eshita unhesitatingly took up a cylinder some twelve feet long packed with explosives, lit the fuse and flung themselves with it into the wire. The bomb exploded, they were blown to bits; but the defences were breached for the infantry to charge through. Two years later a bronze statue to the three 'Human Bombs' was unveiled in the precincts of a Tokyo Temple, having been paid for by primary school children.

The Japanese renamed Manchuria 'Manchukuo', declared it

independent but installed a puppet, Pu Yi, to rule it. Independence amounted to Japanese control of all government and administration. Japanese 'assistants' and 'advisors' ostensibly helping the Manchukuo ministers in fact gave the orders, and the Japanese ambassador doubled as commander-in-chief of the heavily reinforced Kwantung army, whose presence ensured that the new regime stayed in business. The League of Nations sent out a Far Eastern commission under Lord Lytton which returned to write a critical report. Japan reacted instantly: she withdrew from the League, thus yet again isolating herself from her fellow world powers.

The three 'Human Bombs'

Inukai

Its prestige severely damaged by inability to bridle the military, the Japanese government had fallen. It had been replaced by another under an elderly Prime Minister, Inukai, who boldly tried to carry out the Emperor's wish to curb the army's interference in domestic and foreign policies. But the army and navy knew they could act with impunity in the face of governments whose policies they felt were too mild. Premier Inukai himself was shot to death by young officers and cadets.

With him democracy and parliamentary government died also.

The militarists had gained virtual control of the country. Schools were compelled to extend the teaching of Shinto principles of the divine stature of Japan, to foster nationalism in thought and deed, and to give military training.

Despite her diplomatic isolation Japan's trade with the world was booming. But the profits were going largely into the pockets of the industrialists instead of the ordinary people. The time seemed to the firebrands to be ripe for yet another upheaval at home and an expedition abroad.

Children undergoing military drill at school

The explosion at home came in the form of a bloody attack led by junior officers of the Tokyo garrison on elderly and distinguished statesmen, selected because they were not acting 'patriotically' enough in the mutineers' eyes. The mutineers gained no support from other forces, they were surrounded, forced to surrender and the ringleaders were shot. This ugly incident caused some anti-military feeling which in turn provoked the newly influential militarists to strengthen their grip on the country. Japan had already with

Small farmer cultivating rice

drawn from her naval treaties with the Western powers: now she began openly to arm herself.

Japan was, in effect, on a wartime footing and her economy suffered accordingly. Ironically enough the new Imperial Diet building was opened in Tokyo at this time – 1936. It was equipped with every modern facility to enable the two houses of parliamentary government to work efficiently. Unfortunately, this imposing building would for many years house a form of government that was anything but democratic.

National Diet building, Tokyo

It was not long before the new Diet building saw a new Prime Minister move in. He was Prince Konoye, who, as he possessed royal blood, could not be identified with any particular faction. An easy-going man who liked to please everyone, he was unable to control the army. On 7 July 1937, a skirmish occurred between a Japanese patrol and Chinese troops at the Marco Polo bridge outside Peiping in China. Despite Konoye's objections Japanese forces seized Peiping and Tientsin and the following month the Japanese attacked Shanghai, where they soon overcame the strong resistance of Chiang Kai-shek's European-trained forces. Late that summer Japanese troops shelled the British gunboat *Ladybird* on the Yangtze River. The action caused much indignation in Britain but no effective protest, for Japan was now officially an ally of Germany, whom the Chamberlain government was striving to appease. Japanese naval planes also bombed and sank the U.S. gunboat *Panay*, which had on board the staff of the American embassy at Nanking. Japan apologized to America and paid compensation yet once again escaped any more violent form of retribution.

Bottom: USS *Panay*

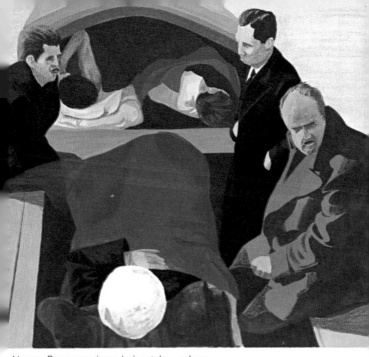

Above: *Panay* survivors being taken ashore

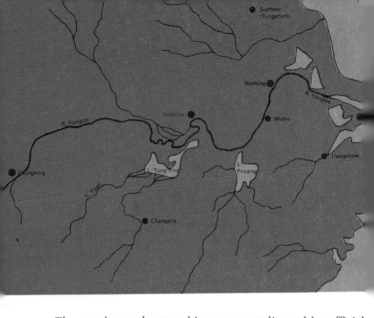

The attacks on the two ships were not dictated by official policy, but were symptomatic of a sinister new streak of indiscipline amongst Japan's fighting men. The war against China produced incidents which shocked the world. The worst was the 'Rape of Nanking'. Japanese forces attacked Chiang Kai-shek's capital in December 1937. After its fall the Japanese commanders gave their men freedom to do as they wished with the ancient city and its people. There followed horrifying days of looting, torture, murder and rape. Foreign missionaries who tried to intervene were thrust aside and even assaulted. When it was all over and word reached the Emperor and government of Japan the commanders and many of the young soldiers concerned were disciplined; but it was too late to conceal that arrogant Japanese militarism was now a menace as sinister as German Nazism.

Instead of asking for peace, as the Japanese had hoped, Chiang Kai-shek made a new capital at Hankow several hundred miles from Nanking. It took the Japanese armies the best part of a year to battle their way there, along the line of the Yangtze River, all the time much hampered by China's flooding and destruction of the land they had to cross.

Chiang Kai-shek

Far left: China,
the Shanghai-Hankow
region

Hankow fell in October 1938; but China is enormous, rugged and in parts almost impenetrable by an army, and since Chiang, now established at Chungking, firmly refused to surrender there could be no question of total victory for the invaders. Instead they faced several more years of stubborn warfare which lapsed into virtual stalemate as Japanese and Chinese in many regions faced each other from consolidated positions and seemed all set for another hundred years' war. Not until she knew that she had lost the Second World War did Japan surrender her Chinese forces and occupied territories there and had to watch Manchukuo and half of Korea quickly snapped up by her old rival in those parts, Russia.

In 1938 Russian and Japanese forces fought a sharp battle on the borders of Russia, Manchukuo and Korea. Some of the more fanatically confident Japanese generals would have tackled Russia there and then but the government was not in favour and the Russians did not desire war either. Although unable to subjugate China as a whole, Japan set up a new 'government' of that country at Nanking under a former colleague of Chiang Kai-shek's, Wang Ching-wei, and declared this the only official administration.

The Western nations were not altogether inactive during this time: nor was there a great deal they could do. Relations between them and Japan for the five years or so leading to the Sino-Japanese war had been tepid. A number of incidents involving ill-treatment of British and American nationals in Manchukuo, Japan and then China served to chip away something of the remaining goodwill. Much resented by the Japanese was British and American moral and economic support for Chiang Kai-shek. When Japan set up her puppet government in China, America that same day made her biggest loan yet to Chiang. Asked to withdraw her aid to Chiang Britain declined. The result was anti-British demonstrations in Tokyo and other Japanese cities and an ugly situation at Tientsin, in China, where British and French concessions were blockaded by Japanese troops and their nationals searched and humiliated. This led to talks in Tokyo at which the Japanese assured British delegates of her wish to keep up their long friendship. Japan's object in China, they explained, was not the conquest of territory but to create a 'New Order' in East Asia with herself as its leader and inspiration, for which purpose it was essential to have Japanese troops stationed at vital points in China. Japan promised respect for the rights of foreign powers and their nationals in China but made it plain that nothing would be permitted to stand in the way of Japan's Eastern Asiatic mission. Britain, preoccupied with the threat of European war, and then with the outbreak of that war, had no alternative but to make some of the concessions the Japanese demanded.

Concerned that Japanese action in China was interfering with American trade there, the U.S. Government gave notice to Japan that she would soon bring an end to their treaty and trade between Japan and America began to decline. A serious new incident involving Russia further darkened Japan's relations with yet another great power. Their forces clashed again on the frontier of Manchukuo and Outer Mongolia. Japanese losses were heavy in the face of Soviet armour under a commander who was soon to become famous elsewhere, Georgi Konstantinovitch Zhukov. Japan needed a powerful friend: Germany proposed herself. In 1936 the two countries had signed the anti-Comintern pact – Comintern standing for

Communist International – an agreement which had further soured Japan's relations with the Soviet Union. Also Germany's mounting dominance in Europe made her seem of all potential allies the most desirable – until, in August 1939, she signed her non-aggression pact with the Soviet Union. Japan then decided that in the absence of any suitable ally she would have none at all. She would stay strictly out of the second great European war, which had now begun.

Zhukov

Japanese possessions during the Second World War

But in September 1940 Japan signed, after all, the Tripartite Axis Pact with Germany and Italy. Emboldened by this alliance some Japanese wanted to attack Russia; others pressed for the seizure of Hong Kong, Malaya and the East Indies. In July 1941 Japan landed big forces around Saigon. When the Western powers objected she protested that she had acted in the interests of the 'New Order in East Asia', and called on America to stop supporting Chiang Kai-shek against her. Conciliatory talks began in Washington between Secretary

U.S. warships burning at Pearl Harbor

of State Cordell Hull and Admiral Nomura, the Japanese Ambassador. But while they continued, a fleet of aircraft carriers and other warships sailed from Japan for the North Pacific. On 7 December 1941 Nomura and Cordell Hull met for yet another session. That same day the Japanese fleet admiral received the expected signal: his aircraft took off and delivered the devastating attack which sank and crippled a large part of the U.S. Pacific Fleet as it lay moored and vulnerable at its Hawaiian base, Pearl Harbor.

The war which Japan was to wage so bitterly, so successfully, yet so ruinously, might never have come about. The Japanese Army – and especially War Minister Tojo – were enthusiastic about it; the Navy, Prime Minister Konoye and many others not at all so. At the last moment Konoye had tried to bring about a personal meeting with President Roosevelt; but Tojo and his kind had stood firm, the moderates hesitated, and then it was too late.

Pearl Harbor was only one of the targets for immediate attack. Bombs also rained on the Philippines capital, Manila, and naval forces struck at the strategically placed islands of Guam, Midway and Wake, quickly seizing them in spite of an heroic resistance by Wake's 400 U.S. Marine defenders. Much of America's Pacific air force was destroyed at Pearl Harbor and Manila and Britain lost the greater part of hers in the first assault. Sent into action without air cover, the British battle cruiser *Repulse* and battleship *Prince of Wales* were easily sunk by Japanese torpedo-planes. But Malaya's fate had already been sealed by the neglect of those who had provided the great island base of Singapore with a pitifully inadequate air guard and with little effective means of repelling an assault from the mainland, which was the way the Japanese disobligingly came. At every point the Allies reeled before withering Japanese attacks. Capable of seemingly limitless endurance and indifferent by upbringing and training to discomfort or death, the Japanese soldier in jungle green pressed on against his ill-equipped, inexperienced enemies. Within six months of entering the war Japan had driven the Allies from Indo-China, Malaya, Burma, the East Indies, the Philippines and many key Pacific islands. To the peoples of these territories she was able to present herself as a sister come to drive out Western exploiters and colonialists. She was trusted and welcomed. All this had been achieved by comparatively small forces – less than a quarter of a million soldiers – spearheaded by air and sea strikes of which the Allies, in their complacency, had never dreamed the Japanese might be capable.

Above right: Allied surrender at Singapore
Right: Survivors of HMS *Prince of Wales*

Australian prisoners of war

The notoriety the Japanese gained for their treatment of prisoners and subject peoples in the Second World War contrasts strangely with their ancient notions of chivalry and honour; yet the code of Bushido was largely to blame. Fearing the dishonour of defeat or capture more than death itself, the Japanese soldier fought until killed, or committed suicide

The fact that Allied soldiers did not practise this philosophy, but would surrender when hopelessly beaten, made them objects of contempt in Japanese eyes.

Attempts were made by the Japanese government to curb these atrocities and persuade military commanders to observe the Geneva Convention governing the treatment of prisoners of war. They went largely unheeded. Faced with the harsh realities of Japanese occupation and the activities of the dreaded Kempei, the terrorist police, the subject peoples of several countries soon lost faith in Japan's claim to a superior role in a united East Asia.

Japanese soldiers in the field were as tough with each other as they were to prisoners. Many a prisoner suffered a beating because his Japanese guard had himself been beaten by a non-commissioned officer, who in turn had been slapped by his officer. The loss of face suffered through an insult or blow could be retrieved by working off the wrong upon one's own inferior, and the unfortunate prisoner came at the bottom of the scale.

Japanese soldier being struck by a superior officer

DEFEAT AND REBIRTH

The spring of 1942 began with Japan in a seemingly masterful position. But she lacked aircraft and pilots. In May a convoy of her troopships and carriers, making for New Guinea to establish a base from which to threaten Australia, was engaged by aircraft from an American carrier force. In the Battle of the Coral Sea seven Japanese warships, including a carrier and seven laden transports, were sunk and many planes destroyed. Perhaps Australia was saved in that moment, for her troops fighting tenaciously in New Guinea's rugged terrain were able to carry on unmenaced from the rear.

Battle of the Coral Sea

The following month a Japanese armada of some eighty ships approached the island of Midway as a step towards an attempt to seize Hawaii. American planes attacked. After four days the remnants of the Japanese force went home having lost four carriers, two cruisers, three destroyers and many aircraft and pilots, against the Americans' loss of only the carrier *Yorktown*, one destroyer and many aircraft. America was building aircraft and training fliers at a far greater rate than Japan. The Japanese had made the fatal mistake of under-estimating the industrial might of the U.S.A. The Battle of Midway resolved the balance of air power in the Pacific and presaged inevitable defeat there for Japan.

Having reeled before the strength and surprise of the blo the Japanese had dealt them, the Allies were fighting ba with increasing success. In New Guinea the Australia inflicted a severe defeat in the Owen Stanley Range, destroy almost the entire Japanese army there. Some months lat when Japan sent a replacement army towards New Guinea i convoy of a dozen troopships, escorted by ten destroyers huge allied air force descended upon it in the Bismarck and sank every vessel, killing some 15,000 Japanese in th days. The Allies were at last able to turn to the attack. August 1942 U.S. Marines landed on Guadalcanal Isla established a beachhead and captured an airfield.

The Marines faced a bitter campaign against fanati

Australians fighting on the Owen Stanley Range

American forces tackling a Pacific island strong point

fenders and had heavy losses before they managed finally
clear the island in February 1943. The capture of Guadal-
nal was followed by a terrific offensive in the Solomon
ands by amphibious forces under the American Admiral
lsey. Everywhere, the Japanese fought with unbelievable
nacity, holed up in bunkers and tunnels from which they
d to be burned or blown out one by one. Few emerged alive.
ey made their attackers fight for every yard of withered
ound and pay for it with many lives. But the Americans
d now perfected the new technique of amphibious opera-
ns, sending landing craft in to ground under a curtain of
ellfire from the big ships. Above all, they held undisputed
ntrol of the air, with the Japanese unable to supply new
ots or aircraft. Though they dared not say so, many
panese at home knew already that their country was defeated.

123

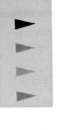

Japanese attacks on Imphal and Kohima

Allied advances and counter-attacks

The India-Burma battlefront, showing Japanese attacks and British counter-attacks

Although Japan had Germany and Italy for allies, both were too occupied losing their own wars to help her with badly needed shipping or aircraft; and as well as the predominant American forces which were attacking her with increasing strength and confidence in the Pacific she had other opponents to contend with. Although the vital road from Burma had been overrun, Chiang Kai-shek's forces in China were getting supplies from the Americans by an amazing airlift across the Himalayas to landing grounds in south-west China. Japan found it necessary to launch an offensive in an attempt to wipe out these airstrips, and met with a good deal of success, but the airlift went on and China remained a theatre in which a good deal of Japan's strength had to be kept in action. A way of destroying the airlift would be to capture the American bases from which the flight over 'the Hump' began in Assam. An all-out offensive here would open the way to Bengal, where Japan's friend Subhas Chandra Bose, head of the 'Free India' movement, assured her she would find immense support from the populace. Many Indian deserters and former prisoners of war had already joined the so-called Indian National Army which was fighting against the Allies.

The break-through to Calcutta could quite easily have happened but for the tenacity of the British and Indian defenders of Imphal and Kohima, who demonstrated that they had learned how to fight Japan's way and win. The Japanese were driven back, encircled by General Slim's forces near the Irrawaddy River in Burma, and hammered into defeat, more than a quarter of a million Japanese being killed or dying from the privations of jungle warfare.

British and Indian defenders of Imphal and Kohima

In June 1944 American forces invaded the island of Saipan only 1300 miles from Tokyo. In October General Douglas MacArthur, once commander in the Philippines, redeemed his promise to return there by attacking the island of Leyte. This provoked the Japanese navy into its last big throw, the Battle of Leyte Gulf, and enormous losses of ships and men. The Americans' immediate objective was to secure more and more bases from which to launch an invasion, preceded by an intensive bombing campaign. The Japanese must be pounded mercilessly before an attempt at an invasion could be risked. Admiral Chester Nimitz moved against the island of Iwojima only 400 miles from Kyushu, in February 1945. It took a month's fighting with many casualties on both sides to gain control of it. Then Okinawa was attacked. Although they did not have warships with which to engage the big Allied fleet supporting the invasion, and were always heavily outnumbered in the air, the Japanese used a new weapon which wrought much havoc amongst the shipping. Taking their name from the 'Divine Wind' which had wrecked Kublai Khan's armada many centuries before, Japanese Kamikaze pilots flew aircraft laden with explosives through a hail of fire to crash them deliberately on the decks of the Allied warships.

Kamikaze attack

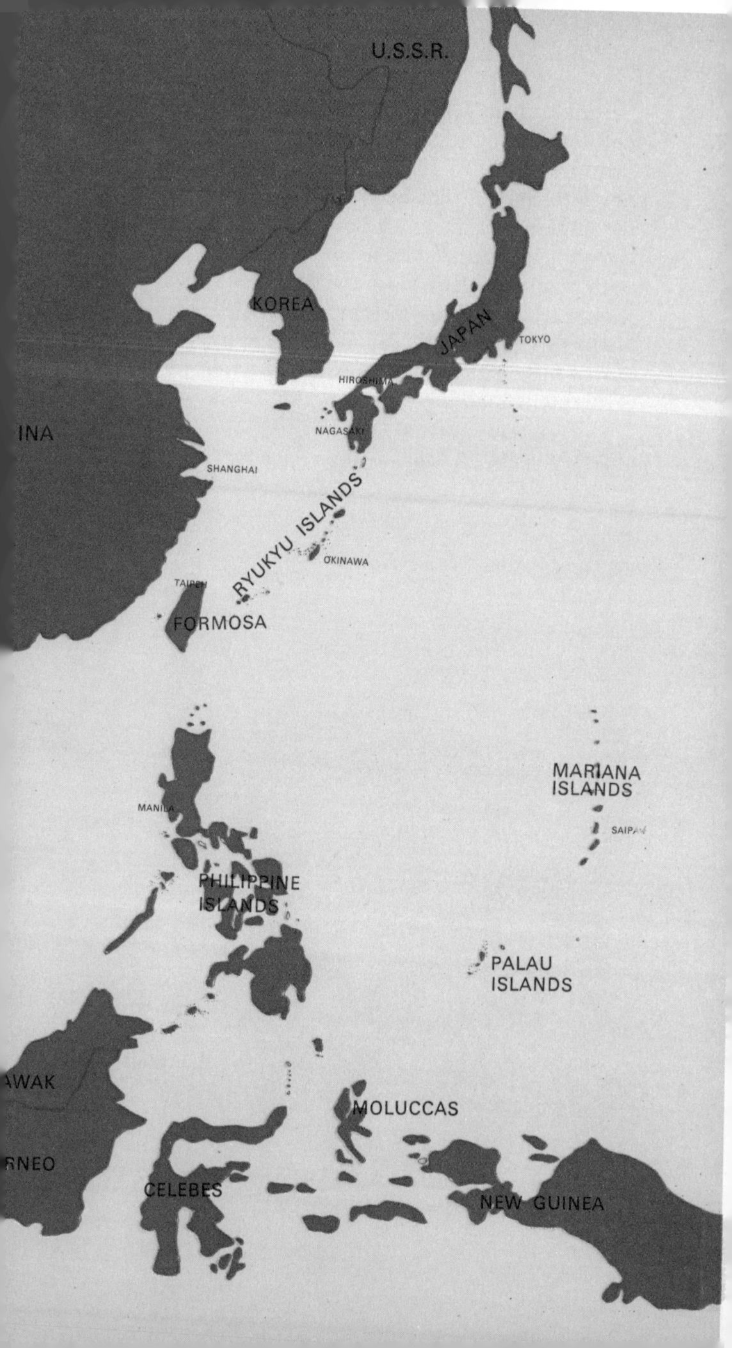
U.S.S.R.
KOREA
JAPAN
TOKYO
HIROSHIMA
NAGASAKI
INA
SHANGHAI
RYUKYU ISLANDS
OKINAWA
TAIPEH
FORMOSA
MARIANA
ISLANDS
MANILA
SAIPAN
PHILIPPINE
ISLANDS
PALAU
ISLANDS
AWAK
MOLUCCAS
RNEO
CELEBES
NEW GUINEA

Hideki Tojo had been appointed Prime Minister short
before Japan entered the war. With defeat approaching he w
seen by many of his colleagues as the man to blame. T
Emperor agreed that he should go, and at last it seemed as
the militarist clique must bow to the moderates; but the arm
which had concealed its worst losses from the public, went
with plans for victory. Its confidence was shaken when Sov
Russia let it be known that she would not be renewing h
Neutrality Pact with Japan when it expired in April 19
On 10 March 1945, Tokyo suffered a raid by 150 B-29 (Sup
Fortress) bombers of the U.S. Air Force which caused mc

B-29 bombers over Mount Fuji en route for Tokyo

damage and casualties than any air attack in history. Showers of incendiary bombs set fire to a solid twelve square miles of the densely-built city, a great proportion of whose houses and factories were of wood. Perhaps 100,000 people lost their lives and a third of a million homes were destroyed. The army blamed the navy for letting such a state of things come about. The navy blamed the army. Their air arms sat tight, reserving their remaining planes and pilots for all-out resistance to invasion. So the bombers came on unchecked and countless civilians died in further raids on Japan. Thousands of others were put into training for a fanatical defence of their country.

On 26 July the Potsdam Proclamation by America, Britain and China demanded Japan's unconditional surrender, in return for which it promised eventually to restore her status amongst the trading nations of the world. The Emperor and those ministers who were already advocating peace moves were impressed; but the militarists, who still held the real power, were not. Their arguments swung to and fro and during the delay a Super Fortress, the *Enola Gay*, took off from the Pacific island of Tinian and parachuted her single bomb on to Hiroshima. It was an atom bomb, and it killed over 70,000 people and reduced an entire city to radioactive rubble and ash.

Two days later Russia declared war on Japan. The day after a second atom bomb fell on Nagasaki. Even the senior militarists had to admit that it was now all over, though younger, more fanatical, elements were holding out. The Emperor took the initiative. Calling upon his people to endure the unendurable and suffer the insufferable, he broadcast to the nation on 15 August – a thing no Emperor of Japan had ever done.

Hiroshima – the bomb and the aftermath

General MacArthur

When Emperor Hirohito broadcast to his people a number committed suicide in front of the palace and there was brief rebellion by some ultra-fanatics. More people quietly and thankfully did as they were told. Their divinely appointed ruler, hitherto a remote figure whom most had never seen, had spoken directly to each one of them as a human being sharing their defeat. They wept. That same day a new type of god was created by the American government when it appointed the sixty-five-year-old General Douglas MacArthur supreme commander of all Allied forces in the Pacific.

MacArthur was soon to take his place in an imposing stone building in Tokyo just across the moat from the Imperial Palace where he would reign in Olympian dignity for some six years as SCAP – Supreme Commander Allied Powers. His aloof mien impressed most Japanese favourably. He had commanded the Pacific campaign which had beaten them: and on 2 September, 1945, he had received a Japanese delegation aboard the U.S. battleship *Missouri* in Tokyo Bay, and impassively watched them sign the surrender document. If he saw fit to cast himself as a demi-god, demanding the adulation of his staff, his allies and the conquered, then he seemed to be justified. The concern of the average Japanese during those early days of defeat was more with what the ordinary soldiers of the conquering powers were like, and what future lay amongst the physical and economic ruins of their country.

Surrender ceremony aboard USS *Missouri*

Temporary housing amidst Hiroshima ruins

Knowing the fanatical reputation of the Japanese, the first American troops to land in Japan at an airfield near Tokyo also wondered just what might be in store. Their anxieties were soon relieved. No attacks awaited them, no suicidal demonstrations; no crowds even. As more Americans followed, then Australians, British and other Commonwealth forces and other nationalities, the Japanese were able to recognize that this first-ever occupation of their land was going to be blood-less and unmarked by acts of vengeance. Fraternization be-tween occupiers and occupied was forbidden by SCAP decree and many exemplary punishments were handed out for disobedience. Yet it was necessary from the outset that both sides should collaborate in the urgent tasks of getting devasta-tion cleared and everyday life running smoothly, while many Japanese were promptly employed by the forces in menial work which brought them into contact with their occupiers. Somewhat to the surprise of both sides, they liked one another and it was not long before good rapport was established and fraternization restrictions unofficially eased.

The wartime Japanese has been likened to an angry sheep. Normally the sheep is the most docile of creatures, doing what it is directed to do and making no trouble towards man or beast. But the rare enraged sheep can be a nasty thing, full of belligerence and heedless of its own safety as it attacks. This in some way applies also to the unsophisticated type of Japanese who met the average Allied serviceman. Brought up under many-sided discipline from the cradle, with an inherited legacy of repression and frustration, and coming in a great many cases from an underprivileged peasant background, he proved capable of bursting out in unrestrained violence at moments of mass hysteria. Yet as many prisoners of war who suffered severely have acknowledged, the sadistic fury of one moment could often revert to a mild, even friendly man almost immediately afterwards. If it had not been so the occupation of Japan could never have proved the largely harmonious affair it did.

Occupied and occupier

Emperor Hirohito in his garden

Many errors of fact and tact were inevitably made by the well-meaning military and civilians of the Occupation whose task it was to restore Japan's economy as quickly as possible. Yet the job they managed to do was a good one, staving off a serious food crisis, reorganizing the government and judiciary through a new constitution, curbing the zaibatsu, the big business concerns. The educational system underwent sweeping reforms and the teaching of ultra-nationalist principles, including the ancient history which ascribed divine origin to the Japanese people, was forbidden. The Emperor repudiated his divine status and tried to abdicate in favour of his son but was urged from his own and the Occupation's side not to do so. With much dignity he endeavoured to persuade the Supreme Commander that he himself should bear whatever punishment might be handed out for war guilt. His selfless gesture was declined. Arrests were already being made – many of them in the form of polite summonses – of men whose personal association with wartime atrocities or in furthering Japan's more ruthless ambitions seemed to need investigating. The date after which acts were regarded as war crimes was set as the 'Mukden Incident' of 1931.

Twenty-eight major war criminals were prosecuted in Tokyo before the International Military Tribunal for the Far East comprising judges from eleven countries. Accused were allowed to be represented by counsel and to testify on their own behalf. The trials, like those of the Nazi leaders at Nuremburg, took an immense time, with the result that the public at large became rather indifferent to the outcome. Seven of the major criminals, including Hideki Tojo, who accepted full responsibility for starting the Pacific War were executed. A number of lesser tribunals conducted similar trials throughout the war areas and some hundreds of Japanese were sentenced to death. It was a just and mild enough retribution for what had happened between December 1941 and August 1945.

Hideki Tojo

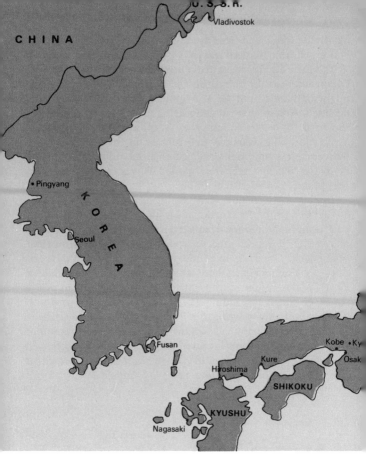

Confident that the 'democratization' of Japan was going on well, and keen to cut down its heavy financial cost to herself, America proposed in 1947 to the other powers that the time had come for a peace conference that would pave the way to ending the Occupation. But by now the Cold War was at a particularly chilly stage and Japan's position could clearly prove to be strategically important. Almost inevitably, the major powers failed to agree upon grounds for discussing Japan's return to independence. America's proposal was dropped but Japan was to be encouraged to stand more on her

HOKKAIDO

Hakodate

A N

ONSHU

Tokyo

Yokohama

Japan in relation to Korea

own feet politically and economically. Consequently, it was not long before the zaibatsu were back on the scene, with SCAP turning a benevolent eye. Japan was allowed to resume international trading and many important men who had been debarred from public office, or influence in industry, because of their wartime activities were able to begin the short climb back to prominence. They were helped by the outbreak of new conflict – the Korean War in 1950 in which Japan's geographical position and industrial capacity clearly had a most fitting part to play as an ideal base and source of supplies for the United Nations force. She seized the opportunity for all she was worth, and prospered immensely. Japan's industry leaped ahead on modernized lines; her big and small traders did brisk business with U.N. troops on leave; money circulated increasingly and the rebuilding programmes of cities was speeded up. As a result, within those few years following her crushing defeat, Japan looked virtually as though she had never been defeated and never had war brought home to her at all.

An event in April 1951 was of great significance in Japanese eyes. General MacArthur, having high-handedly declined a summons by his President, Harry S. Truman, to come and confer with him, was forthrightly sacked. This proved more about democracy than much of the earnest teachings over the years by the Occupation's specialist instructors in the subject. A military demi-god had been seen to be cut down to size by a civilian. They approved the principle but were genuinely sorry to see MacArthur go, not least because crisis at the top level of the Occupation might mean its continuing for more years. They had not long to wait. They had another colourful American to thank – John Foster Dulles, the President's globe-trotting special adviser. His difficult task was to persuade the many other powers with a stake in the Occupation that because America felt the time had come to end it, they should agree. The Soviet Union and her Communist partners emphatically did not agree. Great Britain was prepared to do so but wanted some controls to remain on Japan's economy. Such countries as the Philippines and Australia, vividly mindful of what Japan had done, or had intended to do to them during the war, found it almost impossible to forgive and mistrusted her too much to want the Occupation to end. As to her old adversary, China, the question was, which government – Nationalist or Communist – was entitled to negotiate. With great ingenuity and persuasive skill, not to mention physical energy, Dulles managed to reconcile most of these interests, though when the treaty was signed at San Francisco on 8 September 1951, several countries, including the Communist bloc, refused to participate. In spite of them, the Occupation came to an end, though American forces retained certain bases in Japan, at that country's 'request', to safeguard her security. She herself gradually took over her own defence responsibilities, while 'always avoiding any armament which would be an offensive threat'.

In the windows and doorways of little slate-roofed houses and shops all over Japan the red and white sun-flags stirred in the spring breeze. It was 28 April 1952. The Occupation was over as was the worse humiliation Japan had ever suffered.

The Occupation ends

After the initial period of mutual suspicion there had been little actual resentment amongst the Japanese towards their occupiers. Few outrages had been perpetrated against them, and then only in swiftly-punished individual cases. Many Japanese had found worthwhile enjoyment with the Allies and sincere friendships had been made. Now that the Occupation was over, however, resentment against the continued presence of American troops became considerable. Fanned by Communist agitators, and vociferously expressed by students, it resulted in demonstrations, riots and anti-American campaigns in the press. The most violent anti-American outburst came in March 1954. When America tested a hydrogen bomb in the Pacific the crew of a Japanese fishing boat and their catch were affected by fall-out radiation when a wind blew contrary to the scientists' expectations. Fear that the entire harvest of the Pacific might have been contaminated – fish, with rice, is Japan's staple food – coupled with resentment at an ill-judged and incorrect American suggestion that the fishing boat had been a spy-vessel observing the test, was much exploited by the Left and there seemed for a time a real possibility of a popular swing towards Socialism in Japan. But the big Socialist powers had never been her close friends – rather the reverse. With the highest standard of living in Asia, especially since SCAP's land reform had lifted the agricultural worker to a prosperity he had never known, she had nothing to gain from Socialism, distrusted it traditionally, and now rejected it. Although the moderate and extreme Socialist parties in the Diet combined into one party of impressive strength, the Conservatives followed suit to form the Liberal-Democratic Party which year by year has continued to hold some half of the 486 seats in the House of Representatives and of the 250 in the House of Councillors. Indeed, while other countries' political balances have swung up and down ever since the Second World War, Japan's has remained remarkably steady in favour of the Conservatives. The Liberal-Democrats today are identified in the eyes of most Japanese with Western sympathies and democratic freedom, while the Socialists are seen as sympathetic to the Soviet Union and Communist China.

Above: Bikini H-bomb   Below: Victim of radiation sickness

Much of Japan's magnificent scenery remains today un-unspoiled, timeless, and many traditional customs and courtesies have survived the hurly-burly of modern life. Yet Japanese life is changing and with it the face of Japan. It is still possible to see graceful kimonos worn in gratifying numbers on high days and holidays, occasionally (mostly at weddings) with the complicated hairstyles familiar to Westerners only from pictures and on those charming Japanese dolls. But the kimono, with its tight, waist-encircling obi, is uncomfortable to wear and the classic hair-do is nine times out of ten a wig. The Japanese girl prefers her short skirt, her twentieth-century hair-do. Traditional garb has become for most Japanese something of a fancy dress.

The Japanese home presents more of a compromise. In pre-war days it was the pride of richer Japanese to have perhaps one room in rather stiff Western style. Now the Western influence is apparent in most parts of the house. Many families in the country and suburbs live in wooden houses whose style has changed little down recent centuries and which continue to blend exquisitely into hardly-changed surroundings. Tatami matting still covers the floors and you still take off your shoes and pad about in soft slippers or stocking feet so as not to damage or dirty the mats. There is little furniture to clutter up the space. You sit on the floor to eat and converse, warming your feet in cold weather in the kotatsu, a pit in the middle of the floor in which a charcoal fire smoulders. At bedtime the low table is removed, quilts are dragged out from sliding cupboards and your surprisingly comfortable bed is made up on that same floor.

When you wake in the morning, the first thing your eye falls upon is the kakemono, or scroll picture, hanging behind a delicate arrangement of flowers or twigs in the tokonoma, a small recess which is the honoured place of the house. It is all very Japanese; but somewhere in the house there will be a radio, a television and any number of electrical household appliances. But with the modern trend for breaking up the large households in which several generations of a family lived together increasing numbers of people are moving into modern apartments, furnished Western-style and with only a few heirlooms to recall the things of the past.

Mount Hodaka in the Japanese Northern Alps is typical of Japan's
beautiful scenery

Modern metal vase by
Toyochika Takamura

In the pre-war days when cheap Japanese goods used to flood the countries of the West, often turning out upon inspection to be exact pirated imitations of well-known Western products, one spoke disdainfully of the cheap labour and low standard of living that had made possible this blatant undercutting of our own manufacturers. Now Japanese goods are back with us in vast quantities – but not through cheap labour. Japanese workers receive relatively little less pay than most of their Western counterparts; and they enjoy all sorts of fringe benefits such as extensive company welfare schemes, well-organized, recreation and entertainment and, in many cases, company housing in communities over which the company presides like a firm but just father. The Japanese are hard and conscientious workers and the quality of the majority of their products today is dependably high. From 1945 to 1952 their industry was struggling back to its feet from devastation and bankruptcy; from then until 1959 it was working up to new efficiency; since then it has been rapidly expanding and modernizing, aided by marvellous home achievements in science and technology which have brought an advanced degree of automation.

Since the war the proportion of people gaining their living by agriculture has dropped dramatically. The demand for housing in such cities as Tokyo and Osaka has rocketed. Ways of life and patterns of culture have become markedly urbanized. The West's influence has played an undeniable part. Visitors to Japan who recall a more gracious time deplore the country's 'Americanization'. The long American presence there has left its undeniable stamp; but in general Japan has 'gone modern' rather than 'American'. When Perry forced open the doors in the name of the West, Japan resolved to stifle her resentment and learn all she could from the intruders, one day to be able to copy and surpass them herself. The copying days are now over. In her own right Japan is one of the most dynamic of the nations. The popularity of Japanese transistors and cameras is not only caused by their cheapness. It is also because of their quality which is often superior to competitors.

Space research

147

Japan has learned from other nations, and prospered. Other nations now have much to learn from her. One lesson is that the less money is spent on 'defence', the more is available for industrial and social expansion. This is in no small part the secret of Japan's phenomenal post-war achievement. Firmly demilitarized by the occupying powers she subsequently found herself being pressed by the United States, in the early 1950's, to rearm and bear her share of the Korean War fighting. She resolutely refused and in 1952 stated her position: she would gradually build up strictly defensive forces within a rigid budget which the nation could afford. So far as major strategic defence is concerned she relies upon the American nuclear 'umbrella'. She has been urged to adopt nuclear weapons herself and some Japanese are in favour, especially since Communist China's emergence as a nuclear power. But Japan, the only country to know what it is like to suffer nuclear attack, continues to refuse even to admit such weapons upon her soil.

Demilitarization of Japan has not implied emasculation. The ancient martial arts, as practised for centuries, remain widely popular and in recent years have acquired wide following in other countries. Always it is emphasized that the underlying purpose of judo, karate and aikido is the acquisition of a balanced character and sense of fair play through bodily health and discipline. Nearly half a million Japanese begin to learn judo every year. Karate, whose first principle is 'No attack unless attacked', is of much more recent origin but has become phenomenally popular in Japan as elsewhere; while aikido, the art of overwhelming an attacker within seconds, is claimed to be a great promoter of spiritual harmony and Japanese instructors in it are in wide demand in many countries. Tokyo is a sportsman's paradise. As well as international sports such as baseball (the national game), racing, swimming, golf, tennis, skating and skiing, you can also find Japan's own sports such as sumo. Sumo is a form of wrestling in which after elaborate ritual preparations, very large, fat men try to knock each other down or push each other from the ring by using their sheer size.

National Gymnasium

Most of us associate Japanese manufacture chiefly with such light precision instruments as cameras, binoculars, tape recorders and transistor radios. Her output of cameras exceeds Germany's in size and rivals it in quality. Her watches and timing devices have gained world acclaim and official use in international sport. She has developed many new optical devices for use in science and medicine and on a more common-place level is finding growing markets for her sewing machines, telephones, pianos, textiles, ceramics and building materials.

But the trend in recent years has been towards heavy industry in which there has been enormous investment. In 1950 she was producing five million tons of crude steel a year. Today the figure is forty-eight million tons, and she is the world's third biggest producer in spite of a natural deficiency in minerals. What she makes with the metal provides a long list with ships at its head. Japan is the world's largest shipbuilder in every sense, for not only does her total production surpass any other country's but the biggest ships afloat, the super-tankers of more than 200,000 tons, have been built in her yards. She has held this shipbuilding supremacy since 1956, using revolutionary methods, a colossal achievement for a country with so short an acquaintance with Western practices and so recently crushed in war.

Her motor car industry is the third largest in the world, after the United States and Germany. Improved design and performance has put Japanese cars into a strong competitive position against long-established Western makes and such high-performance vehicles as the Honda Formula 1 have often gained first place on the world's racing circuits.

Japan is the world's leading producer of two-wheeled vehicles, particularly motorcycles. Her New Tokaido Line has the world's fastest trains, which are exported to many countries. Her small aircraft for airline and private use are becoming known for reliability and economy. Economic growth in the past few years has been phenomenal. In a single year, 1959, the gross national product rose by about a sixth or three times that of West Germany, often referred to as the land of economic miracle.

Super-tanker *Idemitsu Maru*, 209,302 tons

Tokyo, razed by earthquake and fire in 1923 and by bombing in 1945, is today the world's largest city, with a population of over eleven million. It is sprawling, higgledy-piggledy, old-fashioned, ultra-modern and exciting. Although Japan's birth-rate is one of the world's lowest it is expected that by the end of this century Tokyo's population will number up to thirty million. Work is already in progress to meet this increase by making Tokyo a vast multi-nucleus city, with a great centre and many smaller ones. Eight major motorways are being built to link the centre with the outlying sub-centres. In the centre itself, broad, fast roadways loop and curve ingeniously around the big new blocks of buildings, enviably reducing the notorious traffic congestion of a few years ago and giving the city a twenty-first-century look which, however, does not sacrifice all grace for utility. The city covers nearly 800 square miles. It is made up of nine cities, twenty-five towns, fourteen villages, and several islands. Though mainly industrial there are also 346,000 farmers in the city, and every year thousands of more people are pouring in. A result of this is Tokyo's terrible traffic problem when cars on the main highways are packed like sardines during the 'rush-awa'.

Indeed although much that was traditionally observed until recent years has now been pushed into the background of swinging modernity, the old arts, courtesies and graces are too fundamental a part of the Japanese personality to be abandoned. In the slickest office block there will be some short-skirted secretary arranging the flowers according to the strict rules of ikebana; the busiest executive will always have time to observe the courtesies of address before plunging into tough negotiation. There are big and discriminating audiences for all types of classical entertainment, from Japan's own ancient forms of theatre to Western symphonic music. Literature, art, film, television all draw much of their inspiration and taste from ancient sources. A nation should not dwell too much upon its past; nor should it throw out wholesale the old in order to give the new its thrusting way. On the whole, Japan has made neither of these mistakes. The resulting compromise has made her one of the most interesting and admirable nations of the world.

Giant ventilators for underground car park in Tokyo

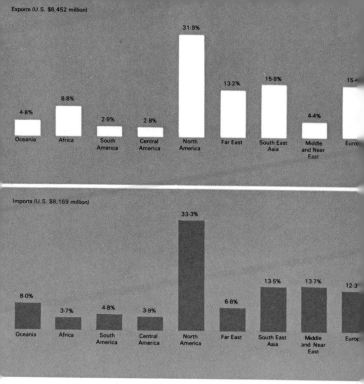

Exports (U.S. $8,452 million)

Oceania	Africa	South America	Central America	North America	Far East	South East Asia	Middle and Near East	Euro
4·8%	8·8%	2·9%	2·8%	31·9%	13·2%	15·8%	4·4%	15·

Imports (U.S. $8,169 million)

Oceania	Africa	South America	Central America	North America	Far East	South East Asia	Middle and Near East	Europ
8·0%	3·7%	4·8%	3·9%	33·3%	6·8%	13·5%	13·7%	12·3

Trade Balance:

Japan could never again isolate herself from the rest of the world and survive. Before the war her biggest market was in Asia, to where some forty per cent of her exports went. Now, as the diagram shows, her export market is divided roughly equally between North America, Asia and the rest of the world. Imports exceed exports, and will continue to do so, for with few natural resources Japan must rely upon bringing in from abroad the raw materials her industries need. Most of them are shipped out again, in the form of manufactured goods which bring healthy returns; but the trade gap remains. Japan today can be said to be the one Asian country that has a high standard of living, and it would definitely be in the interests of the United States and the West to see that this situation continues. The Japanese economy is now far more dependent on

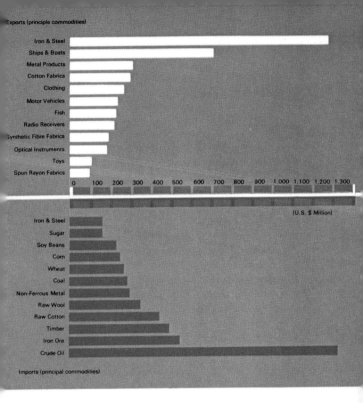

Exports (principle commodities)

Commodity	
Iron & Steel	
Ships & Boats	
Metal Products	
Cotton Fabrics	
Clothing	
Motor Vehicles	
Fish	
Radio Receivers	
Synthetic Fibre Fabrics	
Optical Instruments	
Toys	
Spun Rayon Fabrics	

0 100 200 300 400 500 600 700 800 900 1,000 1,100 1,200 1,300

(U.S. $ Million)

Commodity	
Iron & Steel	
Sugar	
Soy Beans	
Corn	
Wheat	
Coal	
Non-Ferrous Metal	
Raw Wool	
Raw Cotton	
Timber	
Iron Ore	
Crude Oil	

Imports (principal commodities)

the economies of North America and Europe than she was before the war.

Despite strenuous efforts, Japan can only slowly increase her world export markets; and if the United States alone were to restrict trade with her, as some American politicians have been heard to suggest as a measure of protection for their own industry, Japan would suddenly find her economy in a parlous state. Thus the country which demanded she come out into the world and then subsequently bore the brunt of the beating of her is now her chief benefactor. If it were to embarrass her in the matter of trade she could only look Eastward for a market of comparable potential; and that for the West would be more than a shame in view of the developing relationship that has been this book's theme.

155

FURTHER READING, MUSEUMS, ETC.

Examples of Japanese art and artefacts have found their way into museums and art galleries in every part of the world, sometimes in the form of major collections, such as those of the British Museum and Victoria and Albert Museum, London, and the Museum of Fine Art, Boston, U.S.A. Ask the curator of your own museum. Even if you can find nothing on display, he may have something stored away that you can see.

Many libraries, too, have books of reproductions of paintings, sculptures and prints. Books about Japan – mainly text, mainly photographs, or a blend of both – abound and new ones appear every year. To get the 'feel' of the country, *Japan in Colour* by Roloff Beny (Thames & Hudson, London) and *A Portrait of Japan* by Laurens van der Post with photographs by Burt Glinn (Hogarth Press, London) offer an excellent starting-point. A most admirable short history is *A History of Modern Japan* by Richard Storry (Cassell, London) – the present author is indebted to Professor Storry for reading and commenting upon his manuscript.

Older, but still standard works, include: *A History of Japan* (3 vols) by James Murdoch and Isoh Yamagata (Routledge & Kegan Paul, London); *Japan, a short cultural history* by Sir George Sansom (Cresset Press, London); and *Japan past and present* by Edwin O. Reischauer (Duckworth, London).

But every country has its own books about this constantly fascinating land, and your librarian or bookseller will be able to produce a number.

INDEX

157

OTHER TITLES IN THIS SERIES